Praise for

"This memoir by first-time author Ken Libertoff is a gem. It's beautifully written with engaging, absorbing stories presented in a pleasing authentic voice. The essays are insightful and laced with sharp humor, a sense of poignancy, and a zest for life in all its complexities. *Snapshots of a Life* takes the reader on a journey through his life's adventures, challenges, triumphs, and trials, while inviting readers to reflect on their own narratives. This memoir will captivate and delight readers of all ages."

—Howard Dean, former Governor of Vermont (1991-2003)

"Ken Libertoff's poignant glimpses of a life reveal a writer of insight and humor. Whether it's his first job at a Queens bar and grill, bonding with his grandmother over the Brooklyn Dodgers, or a chance encounter in a New Mexico diner, these vignettes give the reader a renewed appreciation of the small moments in our lives that take on significance with the passage of time."

—Rick Winston, author of *Save Me a Seat! A Life With Movies*

"Libertoff's book takes the reader back to his childhood in Queens, the work he did in South Africa to reform their mental health system, and all kinds of escapades in the intervening years. (Including his insistence on taking *real* maple syrup, from Vermont, when he makes his way to a diner anywhere in the world!) It's a delightful read about a life well-lived."

—Mark Redmond, director of Spectrum Youth and Family in Burlington, Vermont

"Ken Libertoff has led a life of diverse experiences and adventures. In this book, he invites you to join him on his travels through settings as varied as Coney Island, rural Vermont, and

South Africa. Along the way, he shares his insights, observations, and encounters. With a combination of optimism and irony, Ken addresses topics as diverse as sports, politics, and home improvement. Collectively, his stories underscore the themes of creativity, resilience, and redemption."

—David Fassler, MD, clinical professor of psychiatry at Larner College of Medicine, University of Vermont

"Ken Libertoff is at the tail end of his seventies, and he is reflecting back on his life. The short essays in this volume are windows illuminating episodes from his childhood in Queens to his present life on a backroad in East Montpelier, Vermont. They are beautifully written, poignant, sometimes nostalgic, and often humorous."

—Bernie Lambek, attorney and author of *Uncivil Liberties* and *An Intent to Commit*

"These are stories about neighbors and friends, loves and lovers, and they brim with empathy and humor. Come follow one life well lived, and get just a tiny bit closer to making sense of what it is to be human."

—Erika Heilman, Peabody Award winner, reporter, and producer of the Rumble Strip podcast

Snapshots of a Life

Rick —

*You are quite a guy —
and Friend —*

Snapshots of a Life

Ken Libertoff

Essays by Ken Libertoff

Montpelier, VT

Snapshots of a Life copyright ©2023 Ken Libertoff

Release Date: January 16, 2024

All Rights Reserved.

Printed in the USA.

Published by Rootstock Publishing,
an imprint of Ziggy Media LLC

info@rootstockpublishing.com

www.rootstockpublishing.com

Softcover ISBN: 978-1-57869-157-9

Hardcover ISBN: 978-1-57869-158-6

eBook ISBN: 978-1-57869-159-3

Library of Congress Control Number: 2023917849

Cover and book design by Eddie Vincent, ENC Graphics Services.

Cover photos provided by the author.

Author photo credit: Jerry Swope.

For permissions or to schedule a reading, contact the author at kenny16@aol.com.

To Sarah Hofmann
My friend, partner, and wife

Author's Note

As I anticipate the publication of this book, it feels like a curtain is about to rise, exposing a stage filled with characters, actors, props, and voices, both loud and muted. As I push the button that raises this stage curtain, it is important to state that my intent is to share my life and life experiences with an authentic voice by crafting, weaving, and sharing original stories and essays that are varied in time, place, and subject matter.

For some, a memoir is best told in chronological order, but following convention is not my goal or style. Rather, it is my desire to craft a meaningful, perhaps powerful, patchwork quilt of essays that results in a compelling mosaic, full of life with all its complexities, wondrous moments, and humbling shortcomings, while capturing experiences that shape and define us.

It goes without saying that memory and recall are subject to confusion, forgetfulness, or misconception. I take full responsibility for any errors in detail or characterization.

On occasion, I have omitted or changed names when they add little to the meaning or content of an essay.

Publishing a book was not something I thought about for the first three-quarters of my life. Yet here I am, ready to share with you, the reader, essays that capture universal truths that should resonate, challenge, and hopefully entertain.

I am humbled with gratitude and honored to learn that everyone has a valued story to tell. I trust that I found and captured my authentic voice in *Snapshots of A Life*.

—Ken Libertoff, Montpelier, Vermont

Contents

Finding Power and Control in Humor 1
Coming of Age at Boggiano's Bar and Grill 8
Atticus 16
From Ebbets Field to the Montpelier Recreation Ball Field . 20
Confronting Challenges and Failure 27
Flying Above the Clouds in Central Vermont 34
It Could Have Been Me 42
A Secret Love Affair Revealed 54
Truth or Consequences. 57
First Impression 62
Bastille Day in Aigues-Mortes 68
March Madness and Basketball 80
The Bush Plane in Botswana 84
I Remember Mama 93
Small World Connections 98
Memories and Life Lessons with Rodrigo 103
My Hawaiian Shirt 112
A Bucksaw, a Scythe, and Silvia 117
The Big Picture on Big Pharma. 130
A Challenging Special Birthday 134
Circus Dreams 141
A Good Eater 148
Adventures in Packwood, Washington. 151
Thinking about Ralph Geer 168
Playing Out the Clock 171
Ode to Jim Jeffords 183
A Booth in the Corner 189
A Boy and His Bike 194

ACKNOWLEDGMENTS 203
ABOUT THE AUTHOR. 207

Finding Power and Control in Humor

I approach my house on a gloomy, cold January day, a little before six in the evening. Although I have had a relatively uneventful day at Far Rockaway High School, a large New York City high school in the borough of Queens, I am hungry and tired. I am also, however, consumed with feelings of worry and dread, for dinner at our house is, at best, unpredictable.

My late return home is typical, resulting from another long and exhausting high school basketball practice. The truth is that I am absolutely thrilled to be part of an exclusive club: the varsity basketball team. I am the youngest player on the roster. As such, I don't lack skills, but I am short on muscle and weight. Having just turned fourteen, I am taller than most, topping off at six feet three inches, but my weight is south of one hundred and seventy pounds, and that would be with my clothes soaking wet. In recognition of my slight frame, our assistant coach who, during a recent scrimmage game, threatened to publicly come out on the court and "kick my ass" if I didn't show more aggressive play, has gotten into the habit of slipping me a dollar a week and ordering me, in a jocular way, to have a milkshake at the local candy store on 129th Street near my house. His suggestion has indeed been my command. His proposal is his way of being supportive, while hopefully adding bulk and perhaps muscle to my frame.

On this day, as practice ends, Coach blows his whistle and the team gathers around. His eyes are bloodshot. Although we pretend not to notice, he seems to not only stash small bottles of liquor in the bottom of his third drawer but to rely on his "refreshments" before most games. His usual ruddy complexion is undoubtedly not from exercise or a suntan from last summer, but he does care about "his boys." With eyebrows raised and with an intense look, he reminds us that a key game with powerhouse Franklin K. Lane High is just around the corner. Coach is not a philosopher, but he assumes a serious demeanor when he admonishes us to be dedicated and to "leave it on the floor."

I already know that this call, a demand, is for total devotion to hard play even if it means an unruly elbow or an undetected push here or there. I incorporate this message like I would a large chocolate milkshake: with vigor and youthful pleasure. Coach is not a warm person, but he takes the time to remind me to crack open my books when I get home. Since he is also my guidance counselor, he knows I am not breaking any records in my early high school academic career.

Basketball gives shape, form, and meaning to my young life, providing recognition and attention. It is a real and imagined companion with hours spent shooting, dribbling, and dreaming. The ball itself is so familiar and user-friendly—especially when it swishes through the hoop. And the very sound of the ball bouncing and thumping is a familiar "call to arms." Best of all is the idealized dream of taking the last shot in a close game and making it as the imaginary buzzer sounds with the clock ticking down . . . 5, 4, 3, 2, 1!

With practice over, we all head out the door. Several of us walk to the bus stop down the street and wait in the cold for the often-unreliable city bus to appear. Finally, it shows up, and as it pulls to the curb, it almost groans as it slows to a stop. It is a good twenty-minute ride home with traffic and frequent stops along the way. With my familiar street in sight, I descend, turn, and walk slowly to my house. Lights are already on in most homes, and I imagine the possibility of a pleasant dinner time with family, and if truth be told, I can see folks gathered in living rooms or around tables. I am jealous.

But as I approach my house, a chill descends. It is not simply the winter breezes but the anticipation of strife, pain, and not knowing how to cope.

Entering the front door, I notice that only a dim light is on downstairs, but a glance up the stairs reveals thin streams of light peeping out from around the edges of my younger sister's closed bedroom door. Karen is nearly four years younger and also carries the burden of trying to cope with a complex and troubled mother. With abandon, I throw my coat over a chair in the living room and drop my backpack and cherished sports bag in a heap. I announce my presence with a loud "I'm home," bound upstairs, and check in on my sister. I can tell from the look in her eyes that things are not okay.

For better or worse, my attention is devoted to my very troubled and disturbed mother.

As I anticipated, my mother is not in her darkened bedroom. She responds not at all to my greeting. I can detect movement behind the closed bathroom door down the hall, and based on recent experience, I presume she is sequestered behind this door. As I have done several times before, I silently approach and try to slowly turn the doorknob, hoping that my maneuver won't be detected. With the gentlest of attempts, I can confirm that the door is indeed locked, which bodes poorly. Standing in the hallway, I feel ever so lonely and afraid.

After a minute passes, I step back from the door and call out, "Mom!" I hear my mother's voice, but it is garbled and shaky, a mixture of groaning, crying, and whimpering. "I am going to kill myself," she shrieks, "I have razor blades, and I am going to slit my wrists!" While this is not the first time I've heard this claim, it never fails to elicit a painful sense of desperation and despair in me. After a minute of silence, she adds more threats and ends by saying mournfully, "I don't care anymore. I just don't give a shit."

I am just fourteen, standing outside the bathroom door, the locked bathroom door, dealing with a crisis, coping with trauma, and dealing with no immediate help or support from anyone. As I stand there, fear and terror engulf me. As if this is not enough, I can feel hunger pangs since it is almost past the dinner hour and I am famished.

This vignette is one of many very painful and harrowing episodes of my childhood but is reflective of conditions that were both crushing and overwhelming at the time. Well into my seventh decade, I look back at my life, especially those formative years, and still wonder how I survived them and how I managed to move forward in life. We all try to make sense of our story, and simplistic as it is, my strength comes from facing overwhelming and, at times, crushing adversity. My quest to survive ultimately evolved from constantly coping with the crippling darkness and despair that comes from being the only son and eldest child of a mother who suffered much of her life from mental illness. I would either be greatly damaged, crushed, and even ruined or learn to cope, be resilient, and persevere.

Two years earlier, in 1957, two events occurred that would impact my life forever. The first is too easily dismissed by those who turn a blind eye to the joys and wonders of baseball. They might not understand how the brutal decision by the Brooklyn Dodgers baseball team to abandon Brooklyn and head west to Los Angeles impacted loyal fans like me. The Dodgers represented the best of Brooklyn and New York, and I was among the millions of kids who worshipped the team. These heroes included the likes of Duke Snider, whose left-handed swing was a thing of beauty; the famous trailblazer Jackie Robinson; Pee Wee Reese, a native of Kentucky, our shortstop who, in a remarkable moment, put his arm around Jackie Robinson before a raucous sold-out crowd in a sign of acceptance of professional baseball's first Black player; and pitchers like left-handed Preacher Roe. Preacher was from some distant place called Arkansas and entertained me and perhaps thousands of other kids with his ever-present mouthful of tobacco and frequent squirts of tobacco juice that occasionally landed on an umpire's shoe.

A much greater tragedy unfolded in November of that year, creating an imprint and shadow over the rest of my life. My father, Bill, a man of thirty-seven, died unexpectedly on an operating table in a Philadelphia hospital. He had suffered from chronic and severe colitis, but a blood clot proved fatal during surgery. His sudden death was an overwhelming trauma for me, my sister, and my mother.

This life-changing event left my mother a young widow with two children, with no employment, and with a neglected disease that years later would be identified as manic depression. The night my father died, my mother returned home from Philadelphia with her brother, my uncle, while several other relatives gathered at our house. My mother was devastated by my father's death. She seemed both traumatized and paralyzed. At the small family gathering at our home, no one seemed to be able to cope with this completely unexpected turn of events, and I recall little or no conversation. The one exception was my Uncle Dave, who lived in Connecticut. He pledged to always be there for me. My uncle was my base of support for several important years although our relationship painfully unraveled by the time I was a young adult in what I considered a brutal betrayal. That is a saga for another day.

I am sure that I did not "process" all that was happening upon my father's death, and indeed, I had little or no capacity to deal with my feelings of sadness and loss. I suddenly incorporated a new identity: a twelve-year-old boy without a father. The funeral was awful, and my mother was out of control with grief and despair, sobbing and frantically hanging on me.

My younger sister, who was shuffled off to stay with family friends before the fateful trip to Philadelphia commenced, now came home, and being together in Rockaway was a step towards normalcy. But neither of us seemed capable of communicating our grief and feelings or providing any real comfort to one another. Those days of late November and December were excruciating and wrenching. To this day, I confess that my greatest embarrassment or source of anguish or bewilderment came when I was finally forced to return to school; no one, not another friend or student or teacher, said a word about my father's death. This silence was deafening. No one had the tools to deal with such a shocking turn of events.

But at this moment, here I am, standing alone outside our upstairs bathroom door with my mother moaning and crying and saying crazy things. While this scenario is not new, it seems different in intensity. As in the recent past, I offer well-meant but probably meaningless platitudes, telling her that things will be all right and that she will feel better soon. Within minutes and out of frustration, however, I tell her in an unsympathetic voice to pull herself together or I will call someone. But I know, and probably she knows too, that no one nearby can help. Her mother, my dear grandmother, lives in Brooklyn but is unknowing and unprepared to deal with this crisis. Besides, she would have no idea how to travel to Rockaway on her own since she rarely ventures beyond the confines of her Bensonhurst Brooklyn neighborhood. I dismiss the fleeting notion of calling the police if for no other reason than because I would feel like a traitor to my mother. I am handcuffed with indecision. I am not sure what is worse: being scared and overwhelmed by my mother's threats to slit her wrists or my inability to know what to do or the fact that I am starved and exhausted.

Then, in one of those defining moments, I happen upon, perhaps stumble upon, a new approach. Rather than try to offer meaningless platitudes or move to a more aggressive or threatening posture, I turn to humor even if it might be dark humor. I don't know it yet, but relying on humor, funny humor, dark humor, self-deprecating humor, and perhaps humor of the absurd, would become part of my psyche and my persona in the decades to come.

Leaning up against the door, I say the following words to my mother. "Mom, I am really starved. Can't you come down and make dinner and then kill yourself?"

As horrible as the situation is, I must admit that after I speak, I feel a certain sense of control or at least comfort in the fact that I've tried a new tactic. There is silence on the other side of the door. A minute or two passes before I could hear my mother undoing the bathroom lock and she takes several steps into the hallway. She looks disheveled, distraught, and slightly crazed, but thankfully, I see no sign of damage to either of her wrists. And I think I detect a wry smile on her face.

Despite all this trauma, she looks at me in a caring and loving way and says some fateful words that contain a jumbled sense of uncertainty, confusion, and assurance. Sounding composed for the moment, she says with a reaffirming hint of affection, "What do you want?"

Coming of Age at Boggiano's Bar and Grill

On many a warm summer afternoon in 1959, I rolled out my trustworthy one-speed bicycle and pedaled to my first job. With each turn of the bicycle wheels, I was moving forward, transitioning from being "just a kid" of fourteen years to a young man entering "the real world," sort of like dipping my toe into the world of commerce, employment, and some unique social engagements. Back then, I was a city kid, and this job brought new exposure to the joys and challenges of city life.

Perhaps this job offered a much-needed sense of freedom along with distancing from my immediate family. My mother, younger sister, and I were still reeling from the unexpected and tragic death of my father, Wilford, two years earlier. This tragedy created much despair and angst, not to mention collective trauma and financial instability.

During that summer of 1959, I worked at a well-known, popular, if somewhat raucous, restaurant called Boggiano's Bar and Grill in Rockaway in Queens, New York. Its setting was superb, for it was situated in the very heart of a vibrant, blue-collar Irish and Italian community dominated by hundreds of small bungalows in an area known as the Irish Riviera—at least by those locals who considered the bar and grill the local watering hole. Boggiano's was directly across from the entrance to the Playland Amusement Park, which rivaled nearby Coney Island in neighboring Brooklyn as a summer attraction for the New York City masses. Playland, like Coney Island, was perched on the edge of the Atlantic Ocean, so bathing suits were considered an appropriate dress not only during the day but on hot summer nights for summer guests who escaped to the Rockaways from the overheated five boroughs. Let it be said that no one would confuse Boggiano's Bar and Grill with the Waldorf Astoria or Delmonico's.

Although I was a shy and reserved fourteen-year-old kid, my six foot three inch skinny frame was an asset in making "connections," connections that counted in my hometown of Rockaway. That summer, my budding friendship with the Boggiano brothers helped to launch me into new challenges and adventures. Louie Boggiano, better known as Big Louie, was a senior at Far Rockaway High School, and at six feet five inches of lean but solid muscle, his claim to fame was his prowess on the varsity basketball team. Louie was a local hero, even if his vocabulary was mostly limited to swear words surrounded by adjectives for those he did not like. Although I was just a high school freshman, Big Louie took a shine to me as we battled during that spring at outdoor basketball courts in hotly contested neighborhood pickup games. Losing a game on these courts was painful if for no other reason than you often had to wait an hour or more to get another chance to prove your mettle because of the crowd of players and the fierce competition. Since Louie usually was one of the captains, he was selective in picking his team. It was a source of pride that he often took me over older players and even over his little brother Eddie, who was my age.

It was Big Louie who spoke to his family about me and set up an interview for a summer job. Frankly, I was surprised when Louie said he had already talked with them about me. I got a call from the bar's manager a week or two later. Given my lack of experience, age, and means of transportation, an old bike, my bargaining power was shallow, actually nonexistent. And frankly, the allure of making money was an attractive incentive.

The very thought transcended any hesitation.

The work assignment was sort of vague. I was to work at Boggiano's at four in the afternoon from Thursdays through Sundays. Initially, I was a rover, ready to do a host of menial tasks that others rejected such as cleaning the bathrooms and taking out endless cans of trash along with discarded food. It was suggested that if I did a good job, I might work my way up to the hugely popular outside concession stand in front of the Boggiano building. The most unusual aspect of my job was the hours; it was presumed that I would work until closing time, which translated to well after midnight every night unless it was raining. The manager, an imposing figure, gave me an offer I could not refuse—one dollar an hour plus tips. When he told me that I would be paid in cash every Sunday, it settled the deal. As visions of grandeur danced in my head, I even went out and splurged, buying an inexpensive wallet, one that appealed to me because it had a small pouch for coins.

Since I lived on 131st Street in Rockaway and Boggiano's was on 97th Street, my commute had its challenges, not the least of which were traffic, summer crowds of revelers, and clouds of bus fumes that could knock you out. I was no scaredy-cat, but you would not mistake me, at that time of my adolescent life, for Charles Atlas, a well-known Italian-American bodybuilder who always, according to advertisements on the back of every popular comic book and matchbook cover, won the hand if not the heart of any number of beach-bathing beauties while brushing aside any number of skinny-marinks who, from the cartoon-size drawings in the comics, hadn't yet subscribed to the Charles Atlas bodybuilding program.

I would not say that I was fearful, but my bike trips in the afternoon and then late at night caused me concern. For comfort, if not protection, I carried on my bike a small backpack-type bag that my older cousin Ernie had given me. Inside my carrying case, I always kept some small change in case I needed to use a pay phone, a lock for my bike that worked only on occasion, and a small pocketknife.

If the trip to work had its challenges during the day, it was at night, well past midnight, that shadows and ghostlike figures seemed to appear behind poorly-lit walls and shuttered stores. And there were plenty of foggy nights when damp but cooling air drifted in from the ocean, further dimming and distorting visibility. Even though the crowds usually had diminished and slowly dispersed by midnight, there were clusters of teenagers, tough-looking boys, and young men, sometimes loud and crude, looking for trouble or for girls or both. My bike bag probably served as a security blanket as I pedaled along, first through the streets and then onto the boardwalk that bordered the ocean for nearly a mile. I did have occasion several times to catch sight of an almost full moon shining on the ocean waves as I whizzed along the almost deserted boardwalk. Some late nights, I seemed to possess informal radar, allowing me to detect any number of couples huddled in beach blankets or settled under the boardwalk. Various images came to mind, a repressed sexual desire was one, but I intently pedaled toward home and some well-needed sleep.

To be sure, I started work at the bottom of the pecking order. Happily, my bathroom and cleaning assignments lasted just a couple of weeks. Without any notice or meaningful training, I was assigned to the popular outdoor soft serve ice cream stand. Things didn't go so well at first. My veteran mentor, an older man with the distinct and frequent smell of liquor on his breath, told me what to do, which was distinctly different from showing me how to pour soft serve ice cream cones. My mentor was referred to as Mr. Feelgood, which explained why I sometimes found his hands touching my body while I tried to concentrate on making perfectly formed cones.

Even now, it is with shame that I confess that during my first week, more than a few of my original cones lost their poorly twisted soft serve ice cream concoctions, which often landed in a messy heap on the ground. When that happened, some sad, sometimes wailing, little kid stood holding up an empty cone accompanied by an angry parent who demanded a refill. I learned that summer that the customer was always right.

But I persevered, mastered the art, and proved my mettle by never missing a day for the first month of work. Nothing riled the manager more than having older key staff call at the last minute with excuses for missing work. On one of those days, I was assigned to the ever-busy concession stand that fronted the bar and grill. At first, I was assigned to simply hand out orders of hamburgers, hotdogs, pizza slices, and corn on the cob. With youthful enthusiasm, I would coat the corn, using a brush, with melted butter, which seemed to be a big hit and was definitely a messy endeavor. I was ever so pleased when one of the older teenage girls who worked the stand mentioned that my long basketball-reach arms were a valued asset in dispensing food in lines that were often six and seven deep. Clearly, I was moving up in the world. Besides, I liked the way this coworker smiled at me when she talked and gave directions.

There were quite a few older, no-nonsense women who were long-time waitresses, but my favorite coworker was a cool guy named Ronnie. He owned a beat-up car, had an ever-present cigarette pack in his rolled sleeve, and sported meticulously coiffed wavy hair that probably was inspired by the ever-so-popular TV series *77 Sunset Strip*. Ronnie could have been the character Kookie in that show, but alas, his life prospects were less favorable since he had dropped out of Far Rockaway High, had an intense Brooklyn accent, had one breaking-and-entering charge, and exhibited a tendency to hit the beer tap in the midafternoon when other staff was engaged elsewhere. It was my buddy Ronnie who seemed to be a world-class expert on the subject of . . . girls. I remember the day he pulled me aside after I had served two provocatively dressed "older women" who showered me with attention. Ronnie suggested in crude terms that they were probably streetwalkers. Although I nodded in manly accord, the truth was that I only had a vague idea of what he was talking about.

The famous wooden roller coaster at Playland, a five-story-high steeplechase, was in direct view of the Boggiano outdoor food stand. It clicked and clattered all afternoon and into the late evening amid screams of joy and screams of terror. Other rides, such as the Whip, elicited strong reactions, and many younger kids seemed to favor the bumper car area. The funhouse was always busy, with clowns, street performers, and countless games of chance. I wondered about the fortune tellers and what went on in their little shacks.

On a Saturday night, as the hot summer sun lowered into the ocean, the noise, the clatter, the laughter, and the endless gaggle of teenage girls in small and large giggling tribes mixed like a steaming pot of stew, augmented by the aroma of cigarette smoke, spilled beer, suntan lotion, and sweat. It was indeed a stimulant for the senses.

As August approached, I had become a small fixture in a larger menagerie of workers. I took pride in wearing my work shirt, the one with the red insignia spelling out Boggiano's in a script design. On a late Thursday afternoon, when things were a little slow, Angelina, an older waitress, told me to check in with the manager. I was apprehensive. But despite being an imposing figure, the manager was direct and, in his own way, friendly, telling me that he and the Boggiano family appreciated my hard work. He specifically said to me that since I had been willing to stay till things closed up late, often very late, it would be perfectly fine, after midnight or so, if I helped myself to any food I wanted at the concession stand before closing it down since I was an assistant to the man who cleaned the kitchen area.

I was stunned. I was joyful. This was probably the best news I had had all year. Given my considerable appetite, this generous offer gave me hope that someday I might replace the muscle-bound and perfectly-formed Charles Atlas even if I was a spindly and gawky teen boy now. During my last month at Boggiano's, as late evening approached, I would begin thinking about my probable late-evening menu, sort of like setting the table of my imagination in anticipation. On many a night, I would cook up a couple of hamburgers, add two layers of American cheese, fry up at least one hot dog and, when so inclined, add a slice or two of leftover pizza. To top it all off, I had free rein and command of the soda taps, the old-fashioned kind with big levers. Did I mention that this was heaven?

Of course, at age fourteen, I knew little of the world, but my lessons in life had surged during my summer at Boggiano's. I certainly could see that hard work did have rewards. And for sure, I learned how pleasurable it was to have cash in my pocket. Yet it also occurred to me that there were several ways of being rewarded for hard work. It was not until years later that I came to recognize that having added job benefits can be most impactful. I may have been paid a dollar an hour in cash, but I can tell you that my benefits package at Boggiano's Bar and Grill, those late-night meals, greatly enhanced my fortune many times over, at least during the summer of 1959.

People like Ronnie and Angelina and the crew of characters at Boggiano's provided me with assorted interactions as we worked together in the summer heat. Not to be forgotten is that young lady, Tina, who, although several years older, gave me chills when she smiled at me and made friendly overtures and comments during steamy, busy summer nights.

Sometime later in August, when I returned to the shed where I kept my bike at work, I found that Cousin Ernie's bookbag, which was kind of dorky anyway, was missing from my bike handle. I had been too lazy to use the lock, I had never used the change in my purse, and the penknife would not even scare the occasional mouse that scurried behind the barrels of garbage at the rear of the bar and grill. This loss, which might have hit me hard early in the summer, was now of little consequence. I had something more important: confidence, life experience, and growing self-esteem.

Atticus

Several years ago, just as the pandemic burst on the scene, I lost a wonderful friend, someone who greeted me early every morning, whatever the season, and who hung out during the day both inside and outside the house. He was like a friendly puppy dog; amazingly, he always came running to greet me as I pulled my car into the parking area down from my house on Sparrow Farm Road.

Atticus, my cat, was a loyal friend by my side through sunny and dark days for more than twenty years. And if truth be told, Sarah, my loving partner for the last dozen years, adopted Atticus—or perhaps Atticus adopted Sarah. Either way, once Sarah moved in, they too were buddies.

I hate people who brag incessantly, but I must state that Atticus was a most charming and handsome fellow. With a masked face in black-and-white coloration, he was like a harlequin character, looking ready to perform in a pantomime play. It would be accurate to say that he cut an impressive figure. I pictured him as a character actor with a top hat and cane, looking debonair and groomed for any occasion. It seemed to me—and with admiration—that Atticus would enlighten any room—usually with a smile on his face—and dance around, especially when guests were in the living room. Settling down, he eventually found a cozy spot and joined the company. All admired his presence and his antics with laughter and applause.

While Atticus was a homeboy, he was known to set out on friendly visits with neighbors near and far. Some families nearby considered him a roving ambassador of goodwill. Others willingly showered him with treats, but in truth, Atticus never shared this information with me. I heard it secondhand.

Atticus was one smart cat. Among other notable achievements, he learned how to enter and depart from our house on Sparrow Farm Road without assistance from the two-legged occupants. Using a small cat door that Sarah rigged up, Atticus figured out that he could push open the side porch's outside door using either his left or right foot. Although I cannot produce a photo to confirm it, I know that, when I finished my daily exercise routine upstairs, Atticus would spend at least five minutes rolling my ten-pound weights on the floor, first with his right paw and then with his left, building up super strength in those impressive front legs.

As I mentioned earlier, at a young age, Atticus, I believe, learned to read. What more proof could you want than to know that he was able to decipher my license plate markings and numbers? How else would Atticus know to run down to the parking area to greet me every time I pulled in? It was a rare day if he wasn't by the car door as I climbed out. This behavior and his greeting never failed to bring a smile to my face.

Now that Atticus is gone, I can share another unbelievable story that reflects well on his intelligence and sensitivity toward others. Over the last twelve years, Atticus shared the house with Sarah's cat, Mr. Jimmy Hendrix. How shall we say it? Hendrix was not the brightest lightbulb in the cat world. Still, the two of them managed, especially in later years, to enjoy each other's company vastly, and these two felines developed a love for playing hide-and-seek with noted passion and enjoyment.

Atticus was a humble cat. I remember the day he received an early admittance acceptance letter to the College of Animal Science at the University of Vermont. He made me pledge not to tell anyone, especially Hendrix, for fear of making them feel inferior. What a decent fellow! Of course, this report is a fictionalized account, but my obvious admiration for Atticus knew no boundaries.

But do not be fooled. Atticus was also a warrior. Frankly, he was, and I am borrowing the words from one of our most worthless past presidents, "one tough hombre." This sentiment stems from an occasion when my kind neighbor, a man named Robert who carried his childhood nickname Stuffi into adulthood, was down in the back field contemplating the prospect of building a wood pile for a future bonfire. Stuffi's daughter, had unexpectedly gifted her pet pit bull to her parents, who were gracious, if not thrilled, about this addition. I cannot remember the dog's name. It might have been Crusher or Bad News, but it's better to let bygones be bygones.

As my neighbor and I shared a conversation down in the back field on a spring day, he had his pit bull on a tight leash. That was a good thing because, within a couple of minutes, Stuffi looked over my shoulder and, with fear in his eyes, shouted, "Oh my god, Atticus is coming over." Sure enough, loyal and friendly Atticus had followed me down the field and made a dramatic appearance. As he drew next to me, our neighbor's pit bull growled, stiffened, and seemed ready for serious mayhem. Stuffi sensed trouble and tried to gain control over his now-energized pit bull. I was paralyzed, uncertain, and not sure what to do. It was Atticus who took the initiative. With little hesitation, Atticus yelped and lunged at the pit bull, who seemed startled. The large and imposing dog retreated and seemingly whimpered in fear. Stuffi and I both laughed in amazement and shared a sense of relief. I walked back to my house, and Atticus, my faithful attack cat, followed on my heels as usual, loyal in protection and concern. The reward for such behavior was a large bowl of seafood kitty chow which Atticus attacked with relish. I sipped a cold beer to celebrate and mark the occasion.

While Atticus attained recognition as a cat that survived the wilds of country living for more than twenty years, he found great comfort in hanging out with us at home. He frequently found his way to Sarah's lap and loved the attention. Atticus also enjoyed sitting right by my computer, seemingly watching my every move. It is possible that he blinked his right eye when he noticed a spelling mistake, which occurred more often than I like to admit, but perhaps I just imagined this special and unique proofreading ability. On a more pedestrian note, he could be found in front of our blazing wood stove on a cold, snowy night, often on his back, fast asleep and probably dreaming of someday having a retirement house in the Florida Keys.

Atticus was not perfect. Some would blame the two-legged adults for "spoiling him rotten." In later years, Atticus took great pleasure in hopping up on our kitchen table, joining us for our meals, and watching intently as if he was a guest at the table. While we put up with and accepted this nonsense, Sarah feigned horror when friends joined us for a meal in the kitchen. "What in the world?" Sarah would say, with disguised dismay, looking at our guests, "I can't believe Atticus has the nerve to jump up and relax on the table as we dine." It appeared to me that Atticus dismissed Sarah's dismay. I could swear that he had a crafty and perhaps guilty smile on these occasions.

Atticus made friends with everyone: my son Jamie, my grandkids Rodrigo and Fiorella, and Sarah's adult children and their partners. He was family in the best sense of the word.

Atticus had a good and full life, enjoying two decades at the homestead on Sparrow Farm Road. He is missed, but his affectionate and heartwarming legacy will remain in my heart forever.

From Ebbets Field to the Montpelier Recreation Ball Field

My grandmother Libertoff—a stern, unhappy, divorced woman—lived in a basement apartment in what is now called the Carroll Gardens section of Brooklyn. The dwelling had no windows, creating a gloomy ambiance. For some reason, the apartment light fixtures seemed limited to 40-watt bulbs. And adding to the frightening atmosphere was the presence of a small freight elevator that went from the sixth floor right down to the basement. Its final stop was not simply adjacent to my grandmother's apartment but opened right into a small back room, sort of a storage space, that I slept in when I stayed over.

Several times a day and sometimes in the evening, the elevator would descend and open with some stranger, usually a burly and unshaven man of ample size, lugging garbage pails or discarded household items through the little room and out a back door.

It probably would not surprise you that I did not sleep well at my grandma's apartment. But when I complained to my mother, she dismissed it with little regard, waving me off, telling me to grow up. Looking back, I doubt that my mom spent much time poring over the advice from noted author Dr. Spock.

Grandma Libertoff seemed moody and troubled, but I suppose that being a divorcee in the early 1950s was a social stain that was hard to remove. Although she taught in a local elementary school, there was nothing warm or tender in her presentation. Even to me, she was cool and distant and was certainly challenged when it came to showing affection.

But she and I had one, and to my recollection *only* one, endearing connection and bond, and that was our mutual devotion to the Brooklyn Dodgers baseball team.

When I stayed at grandma's place on occasional weekends, she took me to nearby Ebbets Field—the Dodgers' neighborhood park—a sacred setting to many. It was a short jaunt from that dark cave of her apartment—a setting that I was already referring to as "the dungeon." Saturday was Ladies' Day at Dodger games, and for seventy-five cents, women young and old would be entitled to a grandstand seat for a mere three quarters. Although these seats were far from the plate and some distance from the action, they were filled with real blue-collar Brooklyn fans who cheered and booed in response to activities on the field, energizing the air with catcalls and adoring commentary while overloaded bags of popcorn and containers of beer were spilled with reckless abandon.

The green grass down on the field was a beautiful sight to behold as our heroes performed. While Jackie Robinson stole bases with reckless abandon and Duke Snider blasted home runs over the wall into Flatbush Avenue, noted fan Hilda Chester entertained the masses with her cowbell and organist Gladys Gooding serenaded the loyal fanbase. And when a Dodger hit a grandstand home run, I beamed with pride when the radio announcer proudly reported that the team was donating cartons of Lucky Strike cigarettes to veteran administration hospitals around the country.

Grandma Libertoff was not a big spender. In all the time we went to games together, we never once munched on a hot dog or a heaping container of fries. Our ritual was to bring peanut butter and jelly sandwiches from home and take them out during the home team's seventh-inning stretch. And added to the game-day menu were carefully wrapped Oreo cookies—enough for each of us to have five or six—and Grandma's thermos of water, water that was cold when we headed out to the ballpark but went lukewarm while sitting for an hour or two in the warm Brooklyn sun. Still, it was better than nothing.

Perhaps to prove my mettle with my grandma, I had my own ritual. As soon as the game ended, I would set out on a hunting expedition in the several nearby trash barrels. Carefully, I would dip my hand into the mess and seek out my prey: recently disposed-of Borden's "Elsie the Cow" ice cream Dixie Cup covers. This was a popular ice cream brand back then, and the Dodgers allowed any ten-year-old kid like me who presented a dozen cup covers with "Elsie the Cow" smiling up at you to purchase a grandstand seat for fifty cents at a future game. My grandmother usually applauded my work ethic but made sure that I washed my hands after fishing around in the soiled, smelly trash bins. She smiled when I held up my collection of valued ice cream cup covers, and that emotional outburst made my day. Perhaps this was her way of sharing and showing affection.

For some reason, I remember often going to games against the Philadelphia Phillies, one of the rival national league clubs. Although the Phillies were generally not as proficient as the Dodgers, they had a great pitcher, a young fellow named Robin Roberts. "Oh, no!" Grandma would exclaim the night before the weekend tilt as she read the *New York Post* sports section, "Guess who is pitching tomorrow? Robin Roberts!" We both feared and loathed this guy. He was scary out on the mound.

Grandma Libertoff and I would sit up in the bleachers and watch as Roberts mowed down many a Dodger slugger. "I hate that guy," I remember saying to my grandma, sounding just like the rabid young fan I was. Grandma nodded in sympathy, especially when Duke Snider, Jackie Robinson, Pee Wee Reese, or stocky catcher Roy Campanella struck out in vain attempts to swat a rising fastball pitch out of the park. That fastball, along with his fluid delivery and guile, led not only to a long career but eventually to an induction into the hallowed Baseball Hall of Fame.

Two years later, in 1957, the Dodgers moved to Los Angeles,

and Ebbets Field was demolished, replaced by a massive collection of apartment buildings. Thousands of kids like me suffered from heartbreak, a condition that still carries lifelong implications if not shadows on cardiac x-rays in later life. These glory days in Brooklyn were over, and my devotion to baseball, which had been so intense and personal, evaporated steadily like the snow in New England as April transitions to real spring.

Sixty years later, fate and chance had me living in Vermont, and you can imagine my surprise and excitement when, in 2003 the sports section headline in our local newspaper announced that Montpelier would sponsor a collegiate summer baseball team. The Mountaineers would be part of a league that included teams from other small New England cities and towns. With eyes wide open, I read that the games would be played at the Montpelier Recreation Field on Elm Street, just a few miles from my house. These young players began to fill a void and repair, if ever so slightly, the remnants of a broken heart.

To my amazement, through subsequent sports articles, I was to learn that one famous former major league star had a close affiliation with baseball in our capital city. And he would be honored at a banquet and given the honor of throwing out the ceremonial first ball once a summer.

This man, this major league player, this member of the Baseball Hall of Fame, was none other than . . . Robin Roberts.

After serving in World War II, Roberts, who had played several seasons of college baseball before enlisting, signed up and joined a semi-pro team in 1946. That team represented the communities of both Montpelier and Barre. The team carried the moniker of the Twin City Trojans. They were a popular attraction, and in addition to the local Central Vermont fans who flocked to games, a lonely baseball scout from the Philadelphia Phillies took notice of the big right-hander whose fastball hit the catcher's mitt with a resounding "thwack." Within two years, Robin Roberts was not only in the big leagues but also the ace of the pitching roster for the major league Philadelphia team.

I was away vacationing for the first couple of summers when the Mountaineers began playing at the nearby field on Elm Street. Still, when it was announced that Robin Roberts would visit Montpelier in 2007, I resolved to get a ticket to the July game when Roberts was scheduled to throw out the first pitch. But before departing to the ballpark, for sentimental reasons, I packed two peanut butter and jelly sandwiches and wrapped them carefully in my backpack.

There was a lump in my throat as I sat in the stands at the Recreation Field and watched this elderly, slightly portly man stroll—with a slight shuffle and a borrowed glove on his left hand—to the mound and toss the ball to the Mountaineers' catcher. It was apparent that he no longer had a blazing, big-league fastball, but his pitch, slightly wobbly and off-center, did reach the catcher's mitt on the fly and was softly embraced. And I instantly thought back to memorable and poignant times of decades ago when I sat transfixed, watching this ace take on my beloved Dodgers.

My reverie was interrupted when I heard one of the fans sitting behind me, part of a troop of friends, guys probably still teenagers or in their early twenties, casually say, "Who the heck is that old guy out on the field." This comment was greeted with the muted laughter and gentle snickering all too typical of young men who were trying to impress some young ladies sitting nearby.

These innocent comments did not go unnoticed. They fired me up. I abruptly left my seat and walked down toward the Mountaineers' dugout. I spotted some old basketball buddies who now helped maintain the field and provide field access and, for lack of a better term, crowd control.

"It is time for me to meet an old friend in person," I announced to one of these volunteers, referring to none other than Roberts, who had inspired fear and hatred in my youthful heart. As I pointed toward the dugout and Roberts, I noticed that he was sitting alone. To my amazement and dismay, the young Mountaineers players seemed indifferent or unknowing of the fact that a famous sports dignitary, a Hall of Famer, by God, was seated nearby. My friend minding the gate onto the field saw that I was serious and opened the entrance to the playing area. The Mountaineers' dugout was just steps away, and I ducked down and entered.

Robin Roberts looked up at me, and I was immediately taken by his grandfatherly appearance as he politely stood and shook my hand. After all, he was a Midwesterner from Illinois. His eyes seemed to twinkle, and besides, he retained a handsome profile and a sweet-looking face. He was much shorter than I remembered as I thought back to 1955, and his body no longer radiated vigor or swagger.

"I have hated you for sixty years, Mr. Roberts, and it is time to make amends and share good times past," I said with emotion as I introduced myself. If he were thinking, "Who is this strange guy next to me in the dugout, and what is he talking about?" I would not have been surprised. But he smiled, perhaps out of embarrassment or confusion, and we sat side by side as the Mountaineers game unfolded. Within a minute, I found myself in animated conversation, and words poured out, gushing like a bubbling stream after a sudden downpour. I told him about Grandmother Libertoff (skipping the part about the dungeon apartment), taking the trolley to old Ebbets Field, the pride of Brooklyn on Saturdays, my loyalty to childhood heroes such as Duke, Jackie, and Pee Wee and the rest of the beloved Dodgers, and even my willingness to scour the garbage pails for Dixie Cup covers. Now came the hard part. Looking directly at him, I confessed my fear, dislike, and, yes, hatred for that young Dodger killer, that nemesis, you, Robin Roberts. He was moved by the moment, and I could swear that tears welled in the corners of his eyes.

For the next hour, we exchanged memories, and he regaled me with stories about playing at this very Recreation Field in 1947 when he got out of the army and about how there were cows and even goats up on the hill toward North Street directly across from home plate, and not a tree on the hillside, and how his success on this very field led to a long and successful major league career.

Best of all, together, we reviewed the Dodger lineup from the mid-1950s. To my amazement, I was able to rattle off the starting Dodger lineup from back then, and in turn, he shared with me his strategy for pitching to each of my hometown heroes. We talked and talked, and not once were we interrupted by the cadre of young Mountaineers players, who were oblivious to the special occasion. He was pleasant, humble, and kind; our time together seemed special to both of us.

Robin Roberts and I embraced as the game ended. "I must tell you," I said to Roberts in a cathartic moment, "I hated you for years since I sat up in the grandstand of old Ebbets Field in Brooklyn but no longer. You are a great guy."

Robin Roberts died in 2010 at age eighty-four. As a tribute, there is a small plaque in his honor by the entrance to the Montpelier Recreation Baseball Field. Based on personal observation, I imagine that most fans today walk by it without even a glance or notice.

But there is at least one local fan who pays homage to his memory.

Confronting Challenges and Failure

Since I was a kid, I have always enjoyed reading the local newspaper. By the time I was nine or ten, I was a loyal and avid consumer of the *New York Post*. Please do not confuse this publication with that other New York City paper, the one with "All the news that's fit to print."

For one thing, the *Post* covered the local Brooklyn Dodgers baseball team with thorough daily detail. Besides, the *Post* knew how to get my attention with screeching headline stories like "Man trips and disappears in a giant meat grinder at Brooklyn hamburger plant." In another part of this tabloid paper, usually midway, there appeared several pages of what might be called, 1950s style pin-up pictures featuring boyhood favorites like Marilyn Monroe or Zsa Zsa Gabor along with eye-catching, suggestive pictures of attractive bikini-clad models. Whether these were the "good old days" is open for debate.

I must admit that the local *Barre-Montpelier Times Argus* is more sedate and limited. During my first several decades of *Argus* reading, after a fleeting glance at the news section like in my childhood days, I turn to the sports pages, which have tried to cover the national, regional, and state scene. Unlike the *Post*, the local news is presented in measured tones—unless you think that the weekly Police Log report, "Dog barks loudly on Barre Street," meets your standard for gripping, sensationalized headline news. As for pictures, I must say that photos of stunning cardinals at a Central Vermont bird feeder have a place but fall short of distant pleasures.

Things change. Since turning seventy quite a few years ago, I still settle in over breakfast with my newspaper. After glancing at the news and sports page, I now gravitate to a different section, the one containing local obituaries. Sadly, I occasionally find a friend, old acquaintance, or local personality on this exclusive list. Perhaps, in some ways, this page serves as an older man's security blanket, offering diverse and interesting stories about other lives, some rich, some poor, and some with long moving descriptions while others are almost painfully terse. I come away appreciating that everyone has a life story worth telling. Closing my paper, I confess with humble embarrassment that I take a silent, perhaps sly, pleasure in not seeing my name on the obit listing.

I have great admiration for and jealousy of people—primarily men, I must admit—who, according to their life capsule in the obituary, "could fix anything mechanical." The paper then records how a certain individual loved to tinker endlessly with car engines, brakes, front axles, and steering suspensions, not to mention the manly virtue of being able to fix a broken chain saw, an old lamp, or any other household device. Secretly, I would immensely enjoy seeing such a description of my life story.

Alas, I have always been mechanically challenged. Back in my youthful days, I even had trouble putting the wings on a ten-cent glider plane, and this simple design only required fitting the wings in place. While some people love the challenge of putting puzzles together, I was one of those young teenagers whose stomach turned when I was challenged with a pile of puzzle pieces. I had little or no intuitive sense of how things could come together. It did not help my confidence or ego when I noticed on the box an indication that this puzzle was appropriate for children between seven and ten years of age. Fixing and adjusting mechanical things like the height of my bicycle seat always proved challenging, especially if a wrench was needed. And my lack of intuitive perception about spatial judgment was further confirmed when I took the dreaded

Scholastic Aptitude Test in high school. My final score reflected my ability to correctly write my name at the top of the first page, which, I was told, gave me at least some points in the final tally. In my case, it proved invaluable.

Being mechanically challenged probably was one reason that I had little or no interest in cars as a young teenager. Some boys in my school in the 1950s were studying car models and changing oil so frequently that you would think they were using it as a salad dressing or hyperventilating over some flashy set of hubcaps. I was happy to be out at the schoolyard, shooting baskets and honing my basketball moves or playing stickball out on the street.

Yet on my resume, and perhaps in my obituary, there will be an account of my one summer work position in the Ford garage in an old mill town, Willimantic, just a few miles from the University of Connecticut campus. It was 1964, and I was just beginning to feel my oats at nineteen years of age. During that winter, I had been a sophomore member of the successful and hugely popular University of Connecticut basketball team.

After the season, our coach, who commanded respect, authority, and unwavering obedience, called me into his office. His tone was casual, but I was worried; he was a smooth operator. Without beating around the bush, he suggested that given my modest grades, I might do well to go to summer school. My academic grade point average floated just above the grade level required for college sports participation. The coach was known to crack the whip much faster than a smile. Yet he seemed to be restraining himself, even snickering out loud, when he reminded me that the previous semester I had only gotten a C grade in a plant science class, which was supposed to be an easy "gut" course. This class was devoted entirely to the art of . . . flower arranging. Weakly, I tried to argue that there were too many "classroom distractions," but at the same time, I was careful not to remind him that I was the only male student in a room with eighteen coeds.

I clarified that I needed to work and earn money over the summer. The next day, Coach called to tell me he had secured a part-time position at the local Ford garage in Willimantic with a decent salary and flexible hours so I could take several courses and have time for shooting baskets in the college gym. Coach did not bother to mention that this was the same Ford garage that loaned him a brand-new car at no cost. Being a college basketball coach at Connecticut afforded many perks, and the coach had connections. I did appreciate his help with a summer position but was too timid and perhaps embarrassed to suggest that this might not be the best placement for me.

Within a day of reporting to work on a late June day, it was apparent that I was like a fish out of water. I don't want to exaggerate, but I had more challenges and setbacks than Odysseus had in his epic travels. I thought of quitting after the first week, but there was one overarching redeeming factor. It was the essential support and decency of the garage service and repair staff. This cadre of mechanics and repair people, local blue-collar men with pale faces and greasy hands, looked past my incompetence with compassion and humor. Even with a string of well-placed verbal jabs that were often more profane than funny, they still had my back. The fact that I was on the basketball team certainly gave me cover, and I was grateful. Everyone, it seemed, from the governor down to the janitor at the garage, was a loyal and passionate Husky basketball fan.

My first major assignment was to serve as a so-called "grease gun monkey" with the focused job of lubricating the undersides of cars hoisted on lifts. It did not occur to me until my second day of work that all my coworkers were men of short stature. I stretched well above six feet and had the distinct disadvantage of having to bend over in compromising ways under cars up on lifts, reducing my accuracy and stamina with the grease gun. Contorting myself left me discouraged, sore, and feeling like a three-day-old stale pretzel. Besides, it took specific coordination to use the grease gun while bent in half, which made for some troublesome results. My poor performance did not escape my fellow workers. My lack of control over the grease gun sometimes led to funny and derogatory commentary as they moved out of range of my erratic undercoating techniques.

My limitations and struggles must have made their way up the garage chain of command, and within a couple of weeks, I was transferred to another assignment, one that seemed like a much better fit, at least on paper. My new task was to manage the gas pumps outside in front of the popular garage. By this time, I had shed my teenage shyness and enjoyed meeting with and greeting people. In fact, I greatly enjoyed chatting in an extended fashion with several teenage customers, usually girls my age. This tendency did not go unnoticed, leading to endless banter and jocular commentary by the service staff.

New challenges arose when customers asked me to "check the oil," a standard refrain in the early 1960s. While pumping gas seemed to be at the upper reaches of my mechanical auto skills, it was unnerving when customers asked me to open the hood and find the oil stick. With embarrassment and a dose of despair, I must admit that more than once, I had to get one of the mechanics to come out and help me find that elusive hood latch or to locate the oil dipstick. This was not my fault, mind you. Back then, various models of cars had different latches and dipstick locations. Now, embarrassed and ashamed, I must admit that on some occasions when I could not find the oil stick or get help, I gave the OK sign and closed the hood, relying on the power of positive thinking and a dose of immature teenage behavior.

Perhaps to highlight my woes, on one fateful day, I jammed the gas hose too deep into the gas nozzle of one of those big Ford station wagons. At first, I attempted to quietly twist and turn the gas hose, trying to release it from the cobra-like grip.

Failing that, I applied more muscle and force, which proved great entertainment for the two adorable young children looking at me out of the back region of their station wagon. At that point, the car was rocking up and down with each pull, creating enough motion inside to provide these laughing children with the same thrill as being on an amusement park ride. Their mother, now out of the car and by my side, did not find it quite as entertaining. Sheepishly, I had to quickly retire into the garage and beg for help from a couple of mechanics. Ultimately, it took three of them to extricate the gas hose. I can only imagine this tale of woe spreading like a California wildfire within the garage and perhaps beyond it.

Days later, and to my relief, the big boss, an avid basketball fan, suggested a new assignment. It entailed working in the adjacent, expansive used car lot. During the humid and warm August weeks, my primary responsibility was to wash every car in the used car lot and wipe them all down to an attractive shine. As it turned out, this proved to be a match made in heaven. Not only could I handle the complexities of this assignment without needing a fleet of mechanics backing me up but, when the temperatures rose to 90 degrees Fahrenheit, I could take off my Ford Garage shirt and work on my summer tan as I sprinkled water over my head.

Despite the challenges at the garage, the events of the summer of '64 were meaningful in so many ways. Even with some ribbing and jokes at my expense, I recognized with affection the virtues of the hardworking, hardscrabble garage men—grease monkeys they called themselves—whose blue-collar jobs and lifestyles lacked social and economic mobility. They could be vulgar and crass, but they were decent and caring to me.

I learned about humility and failure that summer at the Ford garage, and the summer also gave me insight into coping with one's limitations and shortcomings. And for decades since then, whenever I have a car problem, I turn immediately to the best tool in my toolbox. Opening that imaginary box, I find what I need when I take out my wallet, secure a credit card, and turn with admiration to those who are blessed with what I lack: mechanical aptitude and skills in taming and healing our valued and often beloved automobiles.

Flying Above the Clouds in Central Vermont

Sitting in the copilot's seat near the instrument panel of the Green Mountain Airlines prop plane, I had an extraordinary view and perspective as we neared the Boston area, with the ocean meeting land as we glided into Logan Airport. This smooth arrival was nothing compared to the initial part of the trip, which started in early morning from the tiny Knapp Airport in Berlin, Vermont. Late autumn was in the air. It was cold outside with a wind blowing down from Canada. As we took off and proceeded south over the Green Mountains, we were given a morning treat as the emerging sunlight accentuated spectacular views of fading but still engaging fall foliage.

The freezing temperature necessitated specific actions on this cold morning in 1979. With my help, my favorite pilot—Joe, who was on the short list of Green Mountain Airlines daredevils—pushed the small prop plane into the sunlight near the Knapp Airport runway. Then, we retired to the small airport café. By the time we finished a steaming hot cup of coffee, this simplistic but effective deicing process was near completion. To say that this deicing process was "low tech" was not an exaggeration.

"Do you want to give it a try?" Joe asked as he drained the last sip of coffee and consumed the last bite of a sugar donut. I thought I detected an impish smile on his face; he was testing my judgment or perhaps my courage. Behind this banter was Joe's considerable flying skills amplified with more than a dollop of recklessness. It helped reduce my anxiety when he assured me that if the plane did not have the proper lift because of ice, he could abort the take-off and then we could wait until the warming sun completed its job.

Joe and a handful of other young pilots were capable heroes in my eyes. Flying out of and back to the tiny Knapp Airport on an exposed hilltop in Berlin, next door to the city of Montpelier, especially in the long winter season, was a challenge and test of aviation skills. The fledgling airline seemed to rely on a couple of old one- or two-propeller planes with six or eight seats. I wondered why neither sported the name of the local airline. Strange, I thought.

One absurd element of this story is that I had no idea how to fly a plane. I took several trips after I was "elevated" to the copilot's seat before I learned how to close and latch the passenger door properly.

For nearly a year, I was a paying customer on the last commercial air service in central Vermont, and after Green Mountain Airlines quietly dropped the copilot's position—a money-saving gamble, I presume—I often became the invited "guest" up front on flights to and from Boston or New York City.

Perhaps one of the pilots noted my natural abilities on the inaugural flight between Knapp Airport and Boston. I was one of three passengers. Since our little plane cruised at modestly low altitudes, there was ample view of the terrain below. After more than an hour, I began to scour out my window for signs of the Boston area or at least the Atlantic coastline. I yelled to the pilots up front that something was amiss, and when they checked their charts and looked out the window, they too discovered that an error had been made. They quickly determined that our little "prop" was not far from Bradley Field outside Hartford, Connecticut. They took a big turn, and thanks to me and my "natural" navigational skills, we made it to our destination safely if not in record time.

This saga reflects a life, my life, charging forward without a clear vision or direction with some bumps along the way. In 1979, my challenges were many. Most noticeably, I had recently separated from my wife, and we were trying to share parenting with a joint custody arrangement while negotiating the painful end of our marriage.

Months earlier, things had been looking up. I had recently been promised a teaching and research position at the University of Vermont, and besides the prestige, the notion of pulling in a regular paycheck was comforting. The commitment seemed so strong that UVM paid for me to publish a paper and deliver an address that summer at a national conference in New York City under the auspices of the university. They even picked up the tab for my fancy Manhattan hotel room. However, the department head, a young newcomer to the state and university, must have bypassed procedures and academic traditions in the hiring process. Ultimately, several of us academic teaching prospects were put on hold and a freeze was imposed.

By the time the second week in September rolled around, it was evident that the verbal promise of a position would not come to fruition. Not only was my life in turmoil with little solid ground under my feet, but I had just begun to form a new relationship with all its promise and uncertainties.

I had to move quickly to shift directions and find a way to restart my career and employment prospects after finally being informed by way of a registered letter that my promised position at the university would not be filled. Since I, too, was a relative newcomer to Vermont, I had few contacts or local options. Fortunately, during my years in graduate school at Harvard University, I spent time in Washington, DC, and established credentials as an expert on the plight of children who run away from home. This, in fact, became the subject of my doctoral dissertation. While in graduate school, I contributed to drafting national legislation, spearheaded by Senator Birch Bayh of Indiana, which decriminalized runaway youth behavior. It was signed into law in 1974. Its passage created funding for runaway youth residential and counseling programs nationwide and identified a need for experts who could serve as advisors and consultants, especially in rural communities. The fact that I was now living in Vermont added to the perception that I was informed and knowledgeable about rural life and effective social programs mainly focused on children and families.

Within a month, I secured consultant arrangements with two large firms outside our nation's capital. Both companies were eager to have someone who not only understood the plight of runaway kids but had experience in rural America. Both consulting firms were impressed that, when I arrived in Vermont, I served for two years as director of the local Youth Service Bureau while finishing my dissertation. It did not go unnoticed that during my tenure, the Youth Service Bureau secured federal funding for an innovative program called Country Roads that provided housing and guidance to young runaway children.

Within weeks, I had a growing roster of assignments provided by the two national consulting firms. I was able to work from home and travel to sites across the country. During my first year, I was engaged with efforts in such far-flung, remote locations as Machias, Maine, the Fort Peck Indian Reservation in Montana, the small city of Metropolis on the Mississippi River in southern Illinois, the Four Corners region of New Mexico, communities outside Monroe, Louisiana, and several counties in northern Oregon along the Pacific Ocean. Besides the busy work schedule, the opportunity to crisscross the nation was appealing, and I was paid wages reflective of standards in Washington, DC, which dwarfed salaries in Vermont. After several months with no income or job prospects, things were looking up.

My rather unexpected career transformation coincided with the introduction, in 1979, of Green Mountain Airlines, based at our tiny local Knapp Airport. Their daily schedule called for early morning departures with return trips slated for late afternoon or early evening. Since Knapp Airport was less than twenty minutes from my house and offered free parking, I soon became one of the few loyal members of the Green Mountain Airlines "club." It was a relief not to have to drive to the Burlington airport nearly an hour away and then have to pay steep daily parking fees.

Over the year my schedule shifted and changed, but my reliance on Green Mountain Airlines was constant. I depended on them to get me to Boston or New York airports. Then I would link up with more substantial airlines like American, US Airways, or United. This arrangement allowed me to better appreciate the notion that "small is beautiful." I almost always flew home late on Friday afternoons, and once my name was listed on the travel roster, young pilots like Joe would wait for my connecting flight to arrive. It was not unusual that I was the only passenger, so there were times when a weather delay in Denver, Albuquerque, or Chicago had me landing in Boston or New York hours behind schedule. The little Green Mountain Airlines plane would always wait and then fly me back to Montpelier, sometimes in the dark of night.

Back then, all airlines had equal access to the departure runways at major airline terminals. On Friday afternoons, LaGuardia and Logan were jammed with departing planes, and I took note, especially when I was seated in the copilot's seat, to learn that we were twentieth or thirtieth in line for departures. As the flight controller called on planes to prepare for takeoff, I listened eagerly to hear calls for Air France going to Paris, Lufthansa to Frankfurt, or a jumbo jet heading to Los Angeles. It was a sight, seeing these huge jets in front of us take off and then comparing their size to our little prop plane with two small propellers swirling.

Six months after I started my imaginary loyalty program with Green Mountain Airlines, I was sorely tested. One or two larger business entities in Central Vermont decided to try the fledgling airline by having some of their younger out-of-town staff fly to Knapp Airport instead of going to Burlington. By then, I usually sat in the copilot's seat, but with strangers on board, I was a quiet presence. Piloting the plane was a young man I did not know well. All seemed in order as we headed north, but when we were a half hour from our destination, I noticed the plane descending and was amazed when we made an unscheduled stop at the tiny Lebanon Airport in New Hampshire. As we taxied to a halt, the pilot announced that we were low on fuel, and he asked the four businessmen adorned in well-tailored suits to contribute $20 for an unexpected fuel fill-up. Money was collected, and the flight resumed after the pilot stepped out, supposedly to add fuel. The episode left a bad taste in my mouth as did my failure to expose this duplicity.

After a year and a half of such exotic commuting from Central Vermont, I began to consider employment closer to home. Foreshadowing this change was a spectacularly difficult flight home from Colorado. A snowstorm in the Rockies delayed my departure, and I arrived in New York hours late. I was gratified to see my old friend Joe, coffee in hand, who was eager to head home. Having such personal and attentive service in air travel is not to be underestimated, but I noticed that Joe was not his jovial self. He turned to me as we walked towards the departure gate and said, "You are not going to be happy."

It was winter and cold, and snow was in the forecast for northern Vermont. "Your door latch is frozen," he said.

My immediate response, once I had incorporated the news, was to mutter "What the hell?" in a less than friendly tone as a flashing red alert light racked my brain.

"I need you to hold the door shut when we fly home," replied Joe, who did not look any happier than I did. I was incredulous, but trying to calm my nerves, Joe reminded me that at one time or another most Vermonters in central Vermont experience having a car door frozen open, unable to latch, during a cold snap. My mind turned to some old movie where a door opens in a jet plane, and passengers are sucked out into the abyss.

Joe was right. I was not happy as I secured my copilot's seat.

It seemed wise to ensure my seat belt was fastened securely, and I tightly grasped the door, which refused to close or latch as we hit a bumpy portion of the trip. Our little prop plane tossed and turned in the turbulence while I gripped the door handle, but there were moments when the handle pulled away in the howling wind. A few swirling snowflakes entered the cabin. My left arm, straining across my body, held a firm grip on the door handle. My shoulder ached, but waves of terror kept me active and alert.

I can attest that only a genuinely adventurous traveler, not to mention a young pilot, would revel in the experience of landing a small prop plane at Knapp Airport in the grips of a nor'easter snowstorm. With heroic effort, Joe located the poorly lit runway at Knapp Airport as we rattled and shook and descended to the ground. With a thud, we landed and taxied down to a stop with snow as our cushion. I made my way over to my snow-covered car. My left shoulder felt numb, but with my right one functioning, I removed the shovel and began shoveling. Getting the car out with one arm was the final indignity of the evening. Although having to drive down from Knapp Airport into Montpelier and then proceed uphill to my house was no picnic, it paled in comparison to my recent flight.

Two months later, I accepted a full-time job in Montpelier as the director of the Vermont Association for Mental Health. My commute to work was four miles for the next thirty years. A half year after my last flight, my eyes were drawn to a story in the local *Times Argus* newspaper reporting that Green Mountain Airlines, our only commercial air service to Vermont's capital, had suddenly shut its doors without any advance notice. In its wake, it left behind many unpaid bills. The story alluded to rumors that on occasion there were unscheduled stops and passengers were asked to contribute gas money. The article ended with another pejorative update when it implied that the Federal Aviation Administration had never granted formal approval to Green Mountain Airlines. Thus, the state's capital city lost access to commercial air service in 1980. More than forty years have passed, and Green Mountain Airlines has not been replaced, marking the end of an era.

Even now, decades later, I never drive by the Knapp Airport exit without encountering a flood of memories. I smile when I think of my small role in local aviation history as a frequent-flier in the skies above our capital city.

It Could Have Been Me

This may not be a story for the faint of heart. Or for people like me who weaken at the sight of blood. Or for those who are rigidly judgmental about morality and proper behavior.

This tale is a recollection of a moment in time, one that mixes romance and reckless passion with cruel, sudden violence. It includes tender acts of kindness and the fickleness of the uncertain line that sometimes hovers between life and death.

It is not only about one fleeting and intense relationship but also about the uncertainty of random mayhem that marks our contemporary culture, most notably in our country's urban centers where the flash of gunfire, blood, the wail of police cars, and a rushed hospital visit are all too common. Idle words like these become more poignant and focused when one is lying on a blood-soaked emergency room table. I know.

This story is about a time when my life was filled with dreams and hopes and adventures imagined, not to mention grand visions of future achievements. It was also a time of recklessness and sudden passionate relationships that are not always easy to reveal, analyze, or explain. Perhaps I was seduced by my ego and a need for affirmation during the early 1970s.

Most life stories, snapshots of specific times, have some quirky, mundane, or seemingly insignificant aspects. I would be remiss if I failed to mention that a particular bowl of soup plays a role in tying people, events, and a love story into a coherent whole. Whether it adds mystery or comedy, nourishment is essential for the body and soul, especially when prepared, presented, and stirred with love.

The year 1973 found me living in Cambridge, Massachusetts. I was twenty-eight years old, in my second year of graduate school, living in a tiny but cozy apartment in an older colonial-style house, one that had been a large, grand family dwelling but now was carved into numerous small apartment units. The location and reasonable cost made this a particularly appealing "find," especially for a struggling graduate student who valued the worth of a dollar, not to mention proximity to classes.

My landlord, Mr. Ponte, was a most charming, dapper, older Portuguese fellow. He admitted as I signed the lease that the actual rent for my apartment was $140 a month. However, since the dwelling was located on *Harvard* Street, its address alone allowed him the liberty of charging an additional twenty dollars per month. Mr. Ponte was not only a charming, old-world character with a perpetual sly grin but also quite a businessman. As he pointed out, putting his hand on my shoulder for emphasis, having a designated parking spot behind the house was worth —with his Portuguese accent—"Big bucks." And he was right.

The year started in an unexpected manner when my wife announced that she had decided to spend a semester at a college some distance away. We were in a committed relationship, but there were hints already that I was, to put it bluntly, unreliable. Perhaps immature but also fueled by the mantra of drugs, sex, and rock and roll, I was recklessly flirtatious.

I started the academic year living alone, but I did have plenty of neighbors. Within a couple of weeks, I took notice of a striking young woman living down the street. I walked by her apartment and saw her outside on the porch doing some strange exercises, which was my first introduction to yoga. I presumed correctly that she was also a graduate school student because her car sported a special grad student parking sticker. As I walked by her place one day, she was unpacking her car, and I offered assistance. Thanking me, she laughed and said, "Golly, you are tall and handsome." Her comment caused me to stand even straighter as I looked at her and noticed her striking blue eyes, not to mention her well-proportioned body. Stumbling for words, I answered with some banter about my recent growth spurt.

Regina was her name. She and I became friends almost immediately. We occasionally exchanged conversations sprinkled lightly with some suggestive comments that hinted at a mutual attraction. This was a time of alternative lifestyles, shifting values, and the dawn of a "free love" mentality.

Regina was smart, funny, and enthusiastic about almost everything. Her eyes beamed intensely with a radar-like focus when she was engaged. I adored her soft, gentle laugh that flowed easily as it rolled off her sensuous lips. It did not go unnoticed that she had the physical grace and posture of a dancer along with the strength and stamina of a dedicated jogger.

Regina stopped by early one evening and asked if I was interested in taking a walk to Harvard Square, which had ever so many attractions. There was never a shortage of street performers and jugglers, and I agreed partly because I was taken with a young singer named Bonnie Raitt who frequently played on various street corners around the square. As we strolled along, I put one arm around Regina's shoulders, and she responded by moving closer. I was not sure if it was because of the chill in the air or if it was a hint or a signal of affection. The close contact engaged my senses, and I wanted more engagement.

When she suggested that we stop at a nearby pub, I hesitated. I remembered, being a frugal and practical guy, that I had a few cold beers in the refrigerator back at my apartment. It also occurred to me that I was a married man. When Regina's request turned to insistence, however, I gave in. That evening I not only opened my wallet to pay for my own beer but paid for Regina's as well, telling her it was my treat as the waiter collected the bill. Despite knowing that it might be inappropriate or unwise, we returned to her apartment, entered her small but well-appointed abode, and fell into her bed without a word. The next day in the early morning light, I found our clothes in a tangled pile on the floor next to the bed.

We were both contrite and pledged to maintain a more traditional friendship with defined boundaries. And over the ensuing weeks, we enjoyed social time together with a casual and easy friendship with an affectionate undertone. But then, one evening as we were saying goodnight, our lips met and our bodies embraced and we were more than just friends once again.

Regina and I were different in so many ways. She was from a wealthy family in Ohio with a private school background starting at the elementary level. She had attended an elite prep school and graduated from a fancy women's college. Regina was a cultured person, an art major pursuing a master's degree, and apparently, she was a promising artist. This was a world unknown to me although as an undergraduate in 1965, I had taken an introductory art appreciation class at UConn, which I found convenient to mention to her. She seemed pleased if surprised with this news. I did not bother to tell her that I had only signed up for the class because I'd been told it was filled with arty-type coeds who were purported to wear colorful hippie outfits and, according to rumor, sported freethinking values.

Regina was talented and sophisticated, but to my surprise, she embraced my stories about growing up in New York, my troubled family history, life on the streets of Brooklyn and Queens, and my identity as an athlete. These stories included descriptive accounts of stickball and stoop ball games, but she seemed most intrigued by the drama of big city basketball. Her interest served as an aphrodisiac to my senses and encouraged me to tell more. I relayed stories about hordes of players: boys and men, white and Black, brutes and decent types. I spent hours discussing my progression to the high school team and my college career on the basketball hardwood at the University of Connecticut.

The fact that our relationship intensified held mystery, but it was vastly encouraged by Regina's surprising interest in my reports about the colorful world of college basketball. We would lie on her futon, and she would egg me on, asking for stories about the packed crowds of basketball fans young and old, the exciting theatrical aspects of the games, the roaring crowds, and the loud and stirring pep band, not to mention the prancing cheerleaders who were the envy of most of the capacity crowds in the fieldhouse. This was "my world" and I was happy to share it. Regina loved it all, and it even overshadowed my transformation from the jock culture of my undergraduate years to my more recent entry into the field of psychology and my improbable acceptance into a doctoral graduate program at Harvard University.

Even though we spent considerable time together, Regina and I never united over or shared a dinner meal. I was a guy who thought home cooking meant hamburgers and hotdogs with plenty of chips and that dining out entailed visits to the local greasy spoon restaurant with friends. Regina was a woman ahead of her time. My eyes widened when she first told me she was a vegetarian. She introduced me to the term and took the time to explain her diet and how she carefully prepared her meals. That gave me a perfect opportunity to ridicule and criticize that which was unfamiliar. Of course, I just had to emphasize that at our college basketball training table, we had managed quite well with slabs of steak, baked potatoes, and piles of toast with honey. And I could not help mentioning that we, oversized young men with notable egos, were most successful without relying on salads, nuts, grains, beans, and some exotic dish called tofu.

I can still envision Regina standing over her little kitchen stove, with her beautiful hair up in a bun, stirring her favorite soup concoction. Partly to get my goat and partly because eating alone can be tedious, she occasionally offered me a bowl of her favorite soup, her beloved miso soup. On these occasions, it seemed as if we were reading a script that dictated that it was time for me to retreat to my apartment and enjoy what I referred to as some real food.

As part of my graduate school program, I was doing research and volunteering at a runaway youth program in downtown Boston. Already, this experience led me to consider making "runaway children" the subject for my doctoral dissertation. My work in the residential setting was stimulating, and being directly engaged with young teenagers made it intensely real. Project Place, a well-known facility, was in a tough part of the city, but just as tough was trying to help unite runaway children with their families. Too frequently, there was a rupture, and more times than I would like to admit, the call ended with a parent saying, "I'm finished with my child. They can do what they want." Healing deep wounds was not always possible given the country's cultural and political divisions, not to mention family dynamics that were often damaged beyond repair.

One early April morning, I departed later than planned from my Cambridge apartment for my assignment at Project Place. I was behind schedule because of Regina. Describing it that way absolves me of responsibility, but in truth, I was more than a willing partner in our late evenings together. I walked from my apartment to the Harvard Square train station and headed with resolve to the Dover Street station on the T, Boston's subway system. Dover Street bordered the South Boston and Roxbury line. At best, these were troubled neighborhoods, well known as either ghettos or slums.

The trip from the stately Harvard campus and the Harvard Square subway station was short in miles but long in distance if measured by economic status, safety considerations, and cultural disparities. This reality was reinforced every time I exited the train at the Dover Street station. From the bottom of that subway stop, it was less than a fifteen-minute walk to the Project Place residential building, which served as a short-term residence for teenagers.

This was no stroll in the park, mind you. The Dover Street station was part of the old Orange Line metro system that featured elevated tracks for miles. The trains were noisy, and the elevated line deprived much of the street below of sunlight. As the subway car doors opened at Dover Street, the other passengers and I had to walk down to the street level below, which was bathed in perpetual gloom. The old, steep, metal staircase was unusually narrow, so much so that if two people passed on it, both would have to shift sideways in an awkward shuffle. When this occurred, I always held on to the railing with one hand, and with the other, I touched my wallet, reaffirming that it was still in my back pants pocket.

At street level, one was greeted by a string of sketchy business establishments, including two bars, a sad-looking pawn shop, and a secondhand store with used clothes and other random items. I remember the secondhand store mainly because it had a handwritten sign in the front window announcing "Used sneakers, four dollars and a quarter" on the day in question. Several stores with closed metal gates and locked doors were interspersed along the way. Grim and depressed might best describe the scene.

The lights were on in the first bar. Looking through the dirty and cloudy window, I noticed that the bar was open for business and seemed to have a busy start to the day. I checked my watch. The time was half past ten, which confirmed that I was indeed behind schedule for the day. As usual at that time of year, the wind was coming from the east, blowing directly in from the Atlantic Ocean. That meant a distinct chill in the air in early April as I walked to Project Place.

As I passed the second Dover Street bar, the door opened, and I heard voices, then angry words, followed by incoherent shouts behind me. I quickly moved away, but within seconds, there was a distinct noise, a *pop* . . . *pop* . . . *pop*, sounding something like fireworks or—something else.

The next thing I knew, searing pain ripped through my right back shoulder. I instinctively ducked down on one knee but bounced up quickly, terrified that further danger lurked. I arose, moving away from the startling noise. I stumbled as I made my way to the door of the nearby secondhand store. As I entered, my eyes settled on a large, heavy man with a three-day beard sitting at a nearby desk, a cigar in his mouth and a well-worn magazine in his beefy arms. Based on the photos on the cover, I am sure it was not *Better Homes and Gardens* he was reading.

"Call the cops," I commanded in a loud but frightened voice. "I've been shot." He threw down his magazine and, without hesitation, yelled back at me, "Whatta talking about; you're fine, buddy."

I was standing now, and his words gave me a jolt of support and reassurance, which was surprising since his attire and presentation did not outwardly suggest unique diagnostic skills or medical training. And for a second, I thought that maybe I *was* okay. I took my hand and reached back where I had felt the initial sharp pain. As I pulled my hand away, my entire palm was blood red, and I sensed an enlarged area of dampness clinging to my back. Before the store manager could dial the cops, we heard the wail of three or four police cars approaching. They soon screeched to a stop near our location, and several officers with guns drawn quickly surveyed the scene. Ducking down, I peered through the window. Within a minute or two and with no clear action, one cop yelled, "Who's been shot?"

I made my way to the door, hesitated and, as I walked outside, raised my left hand as if I were answering a seminar class question. "Over here."

With several more police cars arriving, the scene was chaotic. I had no specific notion when shock began to permeate my being. With the help of two burly cops, I was hustled to a vehicle parked behind a row of police cars whose lights were flashing. In the confusion, I did not even notice that I was being helped into a *paddy wagon,* a dirty and smelly paddy wagon, rather than an ambulance. To add to my distress and confusion, I saw another person in the wagon's back corner, an older Asian man groaning and bleeding profusely. As we pulled away with a police car siren wailing, a puddle of blood appeared on the floor where the older man sat slumped over in the corner.

Within minutes, we pulled up to the emergency area of Boston City Hospital where a cadre of medical staff was waiting. This facility was a training hospital, and treating gunshot victims required a fleet of specialists. Stretchers were ready, and I was rushed inside along with the bleeding and noncommunicative man.

I remember three things about those first minutes in the emergency room although I am sure that shock, pain, and fear clouded my mind. First, I worried not that I would die but that I would not be able to use my arm or shoulder to play basketball again. The other thing I remember was that as I was placed on a table, a nurse immediately *cut* my blood-soaked shirt off, ruining a new and, I presume, expensive garment that had been a recent birthday gift. The third remembrance, and one that I hold dear because it would be relevant to my work in the health care field in future years, was the utterance of a short man wearing an official-looking hospital badge. He offered no introduction and no encouraging words for that matter. He sported a bow tie and a clipboard and asked me one vital question as I lay face down with blood streaking the table and my future uncertain. "Do you have insurance?" he inquired in a perfunctory manner.

The older victim, my paddy wagon companion, was attended to by several doctors on a nearby table. Even in my dazed state, I could sense furious activity and desperation behind a half-closed curtain.

He expired on that table minutes later, a random innocent victim. It could have been me. Instead, it was this total stranger, someone's father, perhaps grandfather, and loving husband, who was in the wrong place at the wrong time on a Boston street early in April of 1973.

I have little sense or memory of my initial treatment but

felt hands and instruments on my back and heard some brief commentary by the attending staff. After further probing, a young, earnest doctor leaned down and, whispering, told me of my luck and good fortune. In his hand was a spent bullet. "You have a considerable graze wound," he said, adding that the bullet had probably ricocheted off a wall before hitting me, which he explained had reduced the damage. After much probing, cleaning, attention and some additional tests, I was wrapped in a large, uncomfortable bandage around my chest and back and moved to a recovery room.

Around five in the afternoon, I was told I would be released but needed to find a ride home. For a minute or two, I argued that I could probably get home on my own by subway, which was not a sensible idea. In addition to my unsteady emotional state, I had a large bandage around my chest and only a flimsy hospital top that was several sizes too small. My mind was muddled, but when a hospital staff member guided me to a phone, I sat down and dialed Regina's number without hesitation.

"Regina," I said, hiding my actual troubled state behind a super-calm-sounding voice, "I need your help. I need a ride home." She inquired as to my whereabouts. I told her I was near the Boston City Hospital. I presume I did not want to alarm her by telling her I was *in the hospital.*

She responded by telling me, in her slightly superior private school voice, to take the subway since the traffic was awful on a late Friday afternoon. "What are you, some kind of prince?" she asked.

Suddenly I felt exhausted and spent. My super-calm voice was replaced by a rasping, perhaps slightly angry, upset tone. "I've been shot," I yelled into the phone. There was silence on the other end. My bluntness got her full attention. Then I heard a shriek and soft cry on the other end. "I'm on my way."

She arrived an hour or so later. I was in tough shape, shaky, tired, and worried. When she saw me, her face turned an ashen pale white, and she looked as if she might need medical attention. Regina quickly gained control, but I could see her eyes searching as she assessed my condition. Before proceeding to the checkout area, I asked her to hold my newest souvenir: a 22-caliber bullet. Carefully we made our way to her car and headed back toward Cambridge. I remember little from our drive home except telling her, "The other guy died," and adding with sadness and despair, "*It could have been me.*"

She helped me out of her car, and I leaned on her as she eased me into her cozy little apartment. As was her habit, she lit some fragrant candles and then found a soft blanket and a loose sweatshirt to throw over my shoulders. Regina shared with me one part of the story that I did not know or did not remember. The police at the hospital had told her that they suspected that this violence was a random shooting: two guys drunk in a seedy bar, an argument and then a shoot-out on the street. No suspects were ever identified. One person died, and one was wounded on a cold spring day in Boston.

Both of us were innocent victims but one paid with his life.

I was exhausted and listless with little interest in eating. But Regina said she would not let me sleep until I had some nourishment. Before I could respond, she reached for and opened a bottle of Chianti and filled two glasses high. While I sipped the dry, tasty wine, she stepped into her kitchen. I could hear her putting a pot on the stove, and she soon returned with two filled soup bowls that she placed on her small table.

And so it was that on that fateful night, I had my one and only bowl of miso soup.

The inexpensive Chianti was a tonic, but pain and discomfort soon prevailed. The tight bandage made it difficult to lie down. Regina guided me over to her couch and held me in her arms, and I closed my eyes. She put my head on her chest. Within a minute, I drifted off to the steady beat of her loving heart and did not wake up until five the next morning.

At that moment, my future was uncertain, but I took comfort in knowing that I *had* a future.

I never had another bowl of miso soup in all the years to follow.

A Secret Love Affair Revealed

With my seventy-sixth year having arrived in the gloom of January, I ponder not only my past but, with resolve mixed equally with trepidation, my future. Writing memoirs provides an opportunity to make sense of life although, in truth, the reality is in the eye of the beholder. So, with relish and joy, I toil to make sense of a whole, complicated, and grand seventy-six years.

This process has unleashed memories of many achievements along with disappointments and moments of despair and sorrow. Some stories capture a most fulfilling career as a mental health advocate in Vermont; others include tales of love and loving partners, recollections of my childhood on the streets of New York City, memories of athletic endeavors through high school and college, and now tales of tennis. Memories also include family traumas including my father's death when I was twelve and a one-of-a-kind mother who battled major mental illness all her life.

Not meaning to be reckless or shameless, I also have chronicled several love affairs. Some have been fleeting like a shooting star across the nighttime sky. Others reflect a constant passion like that of a tall, slow-burning candle that seems steady and bountiful until, at some point, it flickers out with but a puff of smoke hiding but not negating all that transpired. And with glee, I have captured a most serious romance with truth and no unfortunate consequences.

So today, in the exceedingly early morning light, I reveal and confess to a long-standing, passionate love affair. I am entranced, seduced, and embraced by the beauty and wonder of balsam trees.

After coming to Vermont in 1976, I might have been characterized and derided, mostly behind my back, as a flatlander. I met my first balsam tree on an uncertain date when winter had arrived early. The tree, in a field some distance behind my house, with snow sitting on dark green branches, took my breath away. Perhaps it was the spire-like crown that graced its upper tower like a church steeple or the alluring symmetrical shape that moved my senses.

Visual attractions are one of life's great pleasures, but closer physical intimacy is a necessary ingredient, at least for me. I walked down to that field to embrace my new love interest, and when I did, I was rewarded with a distinct and seductive fragrance that aroused my senses to a fevered pitch. To my lasting amazement, this aroma remains a true and constant secret link between me and my beloved. Like with other love affairs, particularly long-lasting ones, I thought it best to embrace the warmth and glow of affection, partner well, and seize that experience with mutual devotion and without endless time dissecting and analyzing the relationship.

The ecstasy of love drives me to strange and unpredictable behaviors. Starting in the early 1980s. I began a new hobby of sorts, driven by my lust and passion for balsams. I became—and here I expose my roots founded in youthful city mayhem—a tree-napper, sort of like a serial kidnapper except that my prey was small balsam trees growing wild in our northern climes.

First, in nearby Central Vermont locales, I walked the woods and pastures in search of young, impressionable balsams. And, like many a deer hunter upon finding my prey I would—on occasion—carry and even lug my bounty some distance back to my car. Being young and aroused, sometimes I even shoveled out a young, attractive five-foot-tall beauty. If nothing else, this caused some strange looks as passersby spied these trees hanging outside my car window or leaning outside my raised trunk lid. Over decades, my addictive ache led me to forays to the far reaches of the Northeast Kingdom, the climate of which is perfect for the cold-loving balsams that have now found lifelong residence in my yard and nearby fields. I am entranced, but not so the deer, which steer clear, leaving me to bask in my good fortune without unwelcome nibbles on my beloved.

Today, my love affair is again rekindled in the early January morning light. When the first opaque gleam of that shapely outline appears, as night slowly departs and dawn struggles to report, I strain and succeed in reveling in the shroud-like, enticing profile of my adored trees. Over decades, my little conifers have been loved, cared for, well placed, and planted. The reward is visceral.

The view from every window in my house is graced with the balsam beauties that surround it. And once again, I am alive with passion, with the allure of familiar, pleasing aromas, and with the sight of my now-not-so-secret loved ones, who reward my devotion with a special birthday present. With kindness and with an appreciation for the wonders of nature, these stately evergreens have dressed for the occasion because they know and respond to my greatest desire: to see each of them, young and old, greet me with a magnificent mantle of fresh white snow that transforms the long, bleak, January day into my romantic winter wonderland.

Truth or Consequences

"I want the truth," I said, perhaps half-heartedly but with a desire to know the score. We had been living together for a year, and both of us seemed content with "the arrangement." Not knowing when to stop, I added, "I want the truth; is it love, or are you just after my body?"

Sarah laughed. Now that was a good sign. Having a sense of humor is a prerequisite on my imaginary list of relationship-building blocks. Without missing a beat, as she picked up my dinner plate from the table, she added, "Your body."

We seemed compatible in many ways, yet specific differences reared their ugly heads when we traveled. I was on the frugal side, a man who liked the simple pleasures, perhaps more on the rugged, harsher side of life. At the same time, Sarah enjoyed a more comfortable, even luxurious, approach to travel.

This became apparent on our second trip in 2010 to Albuquerque, New Mexico, where we visited with my son Jamie and his partner Mireya. Sarah, who was always fair-minded, wanted to split the cost of our motel. But, trying to impress, I insisted that the treat was on me. My motel of choice was a Days Inn, my favorite local lodging, notably popular with long-distance truckers. Besides a modest room, there was a complimentary continental breakfast with a sensible and reasonable rate of thirty-five dollars a night.

It was not the rustic and cramped quarters that caused some immediate concern. It was the prominent sign on the wall of our room that drew our attention. It listed the cost, item by item, for any room article stolen or misused: Bath towels, two for $15;

Alarm clock $15; Bed sheets, two for $25; Bathmat $7; Pillows $8. Although the television set, a relic of the past, did not look worth $300, that was indeed the price tag. And if you walked off with the small refrigerator, it would set you back $150.

As Sarah took this in, it caused not despair or depression but an uncontrolled fit of laughter that rolled out like a sudden thunderstorm. Tears rolled down her face as she fought for control. Pointing to the sign, she tried to articulate her reaction, but it was hopeless. Finally, as she gathered herself, she said with animation, "Seven dollars and fifty cents for this towel is an outrage; it's thinner than a piece of toilet paper." This commentary caused another round of hysterics. I joined in. At this point, I, too, was having trouble controlling myself, but we did manage to take a snapshot of the "price list sign," which now is a treasured keepsake.

Months earlier, I had accompanied Sarah on one of her business trips. Since I was retired, I had time on my hands and was willing to be her travel partner although it meant facing some challenges of my own. After landing in Orlando, Florida, without hesitation, Sarah called for a cab. "What about public transportation?" I asked. Sarah seemed not to hear. We soon arrived at the rather fancy hotel that served as the conference center. It was a high-end Marriott Hotel. Sarah immediately went to the Golden Key Club lane, bypassing several other longer lines filled with other tired travelers. We were told by the receptionist that they had overbooked the property, but since Sarah was in the Super-Duper Gold Level Marriott Club (I forget the actual name), they bumped us up to a nearby Waldorf Astoria. What Orlando lacked in charm and public transportation was offset by Disney Parks, Mickey Mouse, and countless upscale hotels and hotel chains like . . . the Waldorf.

Not wanting to cause problems, I did not say much about the well-dressed doorkeepers that rushed for our bags at the entrance to the Waldorf or the luxurious furniture and decor. However, when we entered our room, I did mention that the garish chandeliers in our living room and bedroom reminded me of our visit to the Palace of Versailles outside of Paris. The bathroom, too, was luxurious, with a bathtub that was large enough to do laps, accompanied by a basket of lotions and shampoos that were too good to use but might be terrific souvenirs or even future gifts.

It was the breakfast the following day that led to a minor incident. Sarah went off for her meetings, starting with an early morning forum, so I was on my own. I went to the Waldorf dining room, a vast ornate setting with silverware so shiny and heavy that it could be used as hand weights. I ordered the least expensive breakfast option, two scrambled eggs and toast, which arrived with a fresh flower on the plate. Coffee, by the pot only, was extra, so water was my beverage of choice. My $26 breakfast bill caused an outbreak of indigestion, but at least I had the satisfaction of asking the waiter, dressed in some uniform that made him look like a colonel in the Swiss army, if I could see the chicken that laid a $13 egg!

On yet another trip to New Mexico to see my family—my son and his partner, grandkids Fiorella and Rodrigo, and several cousins—I had the idea to treat Sarah to a bit of vacation so we would have some time alone in a romantic setting. Somewhere, I had heard about a unique New Mexico town, Truth or Consequences, which was a couple of hours south of Albuquerque. Using my ever-expanding skills on the computer, I found something unique and different and, in my mind, something that might be long remembered. Since our side trip was to be a surprise, I went ahead and booked a room.

It was not exactly a room. It was an entire trailer, for two nights in the little southwestern town with the unusual name. Besides the change of pace, this special trailer deal included access to adjoining hot springs, which were bountiful in the area. To add to the ambiance, it was located on the banks of the

Rio Grande River, which flowed past the location on its way to Mexico.

The town was known as Hot Springs until 1950. That year, Ralph Edwards—the well-known national radio host of the *Truth or Consequences* game show—announced that, if any locale in America changed its name to Truth or Consequences, it would be recognized and generously rewarded. A yearly festival, with Ralph Edwards himself front and center with a radio program from the anointed location, was part of the deal. Hot Springs not only changed its name but the enormously popular Edwards also traveled to the small city of Truth or Consequences for the next four decades to mark the occasion. This destination was undoubtedly unique.

Driving into Truth or Consequences was humbling. "Sarah," I said, wanting to be positive, "Don't you love the quirky architecture, the art displays, and the jumbled sprawl common to the southwest." Put it this way: no one would confuse the town of Truth or Consequences with the vacation mecca of upscale Santa Fe, New Mexico.

Before we headed for Truth or Consequences, I informed Sarah of my special surprise, two nights in a trailer. I could immediately detect from the uncertain look on her face that she was caught off guard. She nearly dropped her crossword puzzle book on the ground and turned towards me with eyes ablaze. "What did you say?" In a quiet voice, I repeated the plan.

As we took the exit for Truth or Consequences, we followed directions and saw a sign for a trailer park, actually our trailer park. Sarah's pleasant face transformed before my eyes as I glanced her way. A look of horror descended as we both spotted several trailer park residents sitting outside in the sun with bottles of beer all around. Even I admitted they looked like tough hombres who were having a bad afternoon. And I was sure they were not the town ambassadors or members of the town's official Welcome Wagon group. How was I to know that our rented trailer was part of a more extensive, not exclusive, trailer park that had seen better days?

We made our way to the registration desk, and as promised, we were handed the keys to trailer number fourteen. "Sarah," I said, "Isn't this a new experience, something different?" She gave me a funny look in response, with eyebrows raised to new heights. And I detected little enthusiasm. We gathered our luggage and made our way to number fourteen. Much to Sarah's surprise, the trailer was well-appointed in a 1950s sort of way. The space included two bedrooms—which were an interesting if unexpected perk—a small kitchen, and, most importantly, several air conditioners to cool us on hot nights in Southern New Mexico. Although this "love nest" (my name for our suite) was a different experience, Sarah rallied quickly and—rather than pouting or, heaven forbid, walking out—showed a willingness to be a good sport and embraced the situation, and, me.

Later in the afternoon of our first day, we went to the hot springs and sat in deliciously warm mineral waters, which we were told had special healing properties. To cap this adventure off, we took a short walk, just steps from the hot springs down to the Rio Grande River, where we enjoyed floating in the cooling waters like a couple of kids as we held on to ropes that kept us from drifting down toward the southern border.

We survived this adventure together with laughter and good cheer. In its small way, our stay in the 1950s "love nest" became a memorable building block in our relationship. The setting had romantic consequences, but in truth, we never stayed in a trailer park again.

First Impression

On the dawn of my big trip, I entered my kitchen in the dimness of an early October morning. I quickly prepared coffee and walked down to my paper box outside. With eggs scrambled and toast buttered, as I opened the local paper, I gave silent thanks for having a daily and familiar morning ritual. Today would be anything except routine.

To help calm my nerves after breakfast, I took a slow jog down to nearby Perkins Road, ending at a spot that looks out over a lovely peaceful pond with the Green Mountains stacked up behind. I was in a reflective mood, perhaps even slightly homesick already, knowing I would be away for three weeks on an adventure of a lifetime.

On that day in 2004, the first leg of an international trip had me flying from Burlington to JFK International Airport in New York on a midmorning trip. I was then challenged with a seven-hour layover. It gave me plenty of time to walk some distance to the international sector of the sprawling airport for a nonstop flight to Johannesburg, South Africa. This was my first flight to Africa, and even the prospect of a nonstop trip that was eighteen hours and forty-five minutes long did not diminish my excitement or enthusiasm.

This trip was certainly one highlight of my career. I had met Zane Wilson, a leading South African mental health activist, at a conference in Washington, DC, when I gave a talk at a national meeting. To my pleasure, Zane came over to chat and we engaged in a long conversation. As a result, she invited me to travel to South Africa and to serve as a consultant with plans to have me tour the vast country and consult and work with diverse groups including mental health professionals, elected officials, business leaders, and members of community-based organizations.

Zane was a force of nature and assured me that I would be booked on several television and radio shows including *Morning Live South Africa*. I was honored to be invited but challenged to the core. While I was confident that I would learn a lot about South Africa, the more nagging concern was whether I could provide help and expertise to a country so different from ours.

After nearly nineteen hours in the air, I walked, perhaps stumbled, into the Johannesburg airport. I was dazed, tired, and more than slightly overwhelmed. The airport was filled with people from all over the world, many dressed in colorful clothes from Africa, the Middle East, and other distant ports. To add to the ambiance, small groups—families, I presumed—were cooking on small indoor stoves, preparing unfamiliar but aromatic dishes right inside the airport. A bearded man provided further stimulation. He appeared to be a sheik from a Middle Eastern country who walked nearby dressed in a white robe and headscarf and followed by an entourage of face-veiled women. Trying to gain my equilibrium, I quickly resolved that I was a stranger in a strange land.

I stood in line for nearly an hour as I made my way slowly through customs. It gave me an opportunity to study the social drama around me. Armed with my American passport, I was finally stamped and approved. I entered the central terminal where I was greeted by Roshni, a young woman of Indian descent who was one administrative leader of my host organization in South Africa. The previous year, I had met her in Washington, DC, and was immediately taken by her warmth and supportive attitude. Besides, she had a lovely English voice filled with good cheer. I smiled when she replied, "My pleasure," to my many questions and inquiries.

During my entire stay, Roshni's attentiveness and personal

warmth reminded me how small acts of kindness are significantly valued, especially when someone is exposed to new and different cultures and surroundings. My emotions were close to the surface: excitement, confusion, and overload. It was apparent as we drove away from the airport that I was going to have a unique life experience. I knew, as Roshni skillfully weaved through traffic in bustling Johannesburg, that I was far from the comfort, routine, and familiarity of daily life on State and Main streets in downtown Montpelier.

We pulled into my hotel around five in the afternoon. Only then did Roshni tell me that, in a burst of enthusiasm, Zane had arranged for a small dinner party that very evening so her key staff people could meet me. I sensed that Zane was a woman of tremendous vitality and energy. One did not easily say "no" to her, so I dutifully showered and shaved. I was operating on adrenaline, but my tank was almost empty after twenty-four hours of travel from my house in Vermont. Fortunately, two glasses of South African wine gave me the strength to engage in conversation, meet with and greet people, and provide a brief outline of my work in Vermont.

I only had a few hours of sleep before Roshni called my room early the following morning and reminded me that my welcoming breakfast meeting would begin promptly at eight. Given the extensive travel and time changes, my internal clock was in serious disrepair. But Zane had informed me prior to my visit that I was scheduled to meet and address a group of some fifty or so mental health, business, and political leaders, and I thanked Roshni for the reminder. It was implied that this gathering represented a cluster of influential and powerful leaders.

In honor of my first formal presentation, I dressed in my best and only summer sports jacket, a new and somewhat stiff white shirt, and a tie with the official Vermont insignia. I even made a fleeting attempt at taming my hair.

Leaving my room, I headed down the hall to the elevator. I pressed the "down" button. Nothing happened immediately. Standing in the hallway alone, I had a quiet moment to consider the magnitude and challenge of this adventure. Going down to the first floor from the sixth paled considerably from the travels and travails of the past day and a half when I flew well over nine thousand miles.

The hotel elevator door opened, and I pushed the button for the lobby. The elevator started its descent. Since I was the only passenger, I checked my tie and general attire in the elevator mirror while thinking that "First impressions are important."

With a sudden lurch, the elevator stopped somewhere between the fourth and third floors. For a moment, I took little notice. Then I pushed the lobby button again. I waited. Nothing happened. After several minutes, I began to experience slight discomfort in the pit of my stomach. With each minute, a creeping feeling of panic and claustrophobia invaded my being.

Matters were made worse when I glanced at my watch. It was already a little past eight. Getting desperate, I started knocking gently on the heavy elevator door. I felt foolish. But nothing happened. After another minute or two, I loosened and removed my tie and wiped my brow, which was now damp. Glancing at my watch, it pained me to see it was nearly seven minutes past eight. My only recourse was to start pounding on the door, although it occurred to me that my pounding and yelling "help" might not be the best way to introduce myself to the people of South Africa.

Another five minutes passed without relief, until I detected some muted noises in the elevator shaft. Soon I could vaguely make out voices, but their language was foreign. There was some shuffling in the rear of the elevator, and slowly a relatively narrow opening appeared, and two very slim and very dark African men came into view. With considerable effort, they pried open the door a little wider from the back with just enough room for me to wiggle through. Using arms as pointers, they guided me into a dark, smelly, dirty, and dim elevator shaft. I could hardly see, and I had no idea how to proceed. Following my guides, I stepped carefully, but I also had to crawl on my hands and knees since low-hanging rafters posed severe threats to someone well over six feet in height. The fact that it was summer in South Africa made the interior of the elevator shaft extremely warm.

Moving slowly, mostly crawling, we finally reached what appeared, in the dark gloom, to be a small door. One of my African saviors pushed it open with his feet. It led to a space in the third-floor hallway. Feeling relief and gratitude, I shook hands with my two rescuers, but verbal communication was impossible for they only spoke in the Zulu dialect. I did notice a sign for a different third-floor elevator but decided that taking the staircase down to the lobby was more to my liking.

As I entered the breakfast meeting room, executive director Zane Wilson, one of the truly brilliant, resourceful, and determined South African mental health leaders, was at the breakfast room microphone. When she saw me, she stopped and announced, with a flourish, that "Our guest from America has arrived." She rushed over and, with eyes wide, inspected my rather unique appearance—a cocktail of dirt, soot, and sweat—and quickly heard, in short summary form, my tale of woe.

I was sporting a rumpled, filthy white shirt, my jacket was beyond repair, and my pants had a small rip by my right knee. My hands and face were covered with dirt and grime, and my shirt was soaked in sweat.

Not missing a beat, Zane started her introduction by reminding the audience of my long travels from the remote province of Vermont in America to Johannesburg, South Africa's largest city. With a dramatic but humorous flair, she explained that the last part of my trip, from the fifth floor to our breakfast room, was perhaps my greatest challenge. As I came forward, she handed me a small towel and motioned to the microphone.

As I made my way to the podium, I was at my wit's end but was able to pull myself together. Before saying a word, I wiped my hands and proceeded. With a straight face, I introduced myself with these understated words, "I guess you only get one chance to make a first impression."

Laughter filled the room, and my adventures, big and small, were off to a rousing start.

Bastille Day in Aigues-Mortes

My partner Gabrielle and I enjoyed several summer trips to Germany during the early years of our relationship. With each visit, we managed to go on various adventures—side trips from our base in Germany to Greece, Holland, Austria, and France. In 1986, we set off on a car tour of southern France to explore the Provence region, traveling first over mountains as we slowly made our way to the coast and the lovely Mediterranean.

The city of Darmstadt was the home of Gabrielle's family. Gabrielle, who had only found her way to America in early adult life, highly valued these reunions, and my presence added new dimensions and challenges. Visiting for her was more than travel: it was a return home. It was an exciting experience for me but introduced some complex historical and cultural differences that could not be ignored. Growing up in a Jewish family in New York City as World War II ended, surrounded by orthodox grandparents in nearby Brooklyn, made going to Germany a trip up, over, and around the devastating memories of the Holocaust.

Gabrielle's father was a retired university engineering professor. His life was turned upside down when he was drafted in the early stages of World War II. He fought on the Russian front for the defeated German army and then walked home to begin life anew. As we spent time together, I found him to be a formal older man, a reserved and contained individual. Gabrielle's mother was more engaging and approachable. She radiated a sense of welcome and warmth, punctuated with an endearing smile. She showered me with attention, expressing her affection by preparing delicious meals, especially homemade Wiener schnitzel. I reciprocated with flowers and her favorite cookies. Our mutual affection elevated with each visit.

Neither of Gabrielle's parents spoke English, which was challenging and made no easier by my limited, almost nonexistent German. Gabrielle was the official "translator" in this family construct, and she carried out the task with grace and good cheer although, to this day, I think she modified some of my observations and stories to keep everyone in good cheer.

One way Gabrielle's father did express his affection was by lending us his beloved and ancient BMW motor car. Since Gabrielle's elderly parents had driven little in recent years, the car was a splendid antique in good working order. As I was to learn, despite its advanced age and many years in operation, it performed quite well. On the famous German Autobahn, I cranked it up to over one hundred miles an hour as I tried in vain to keep up with the traffic flow. It was me, not the car, that restrained its performance.

On the morning of our departure from the family home, Gabrielle's father handed over the car key to us, and I could sense his great affection for his beloved vehicle. With the precision and detail of an engineer, he reviewed the car's operating systems and even described a few quirks common to a vintage automobile.

Our destination in the summer of 1986 was the beautiful Provence region in the south of France. Gabrielle mapped out our itinerary and included some exciting diversions. The Fourth of July found us staying in Colmar, a lovely French town on the border with Germany in the Alsace area. Not only was this wine country, but Colmar sported cobblestone streets and medieval buildings.

Colmar was also the hometown of Frederic Bartholdi, the creator and sculptor of the Statue of Liberty. By chance, we toured his house, now a museum, on America's Independence Day, and to my surprise, I became overcome with emotion. Part of my reaction was homesickness, missing my country and especially my young son Jamie. But I was also stirred by patriotism enhanced by the museum's old photographs of the statue being assembled in the New York City harbor prior to the celebration of its installation. This moment challenged me. I was faced with bridging cultures and history far from home.

The next day, cruising along country roads, we proceeded deep into the Provence region. The beauty and the tranquility of many cities and villages, including Avignon, Nimes, and the hill towns of Les Beau and Luberon, moved us. We fell in love with the countryside, especially the beautiful pottery the region produced. Gabrielle, a careful but savvy shopper, purchased several medium-sized pottery jugs that she was sure would look "at home" in our Vermont farmhouse. I admired them too but worried more about the difficulty of getting them safely back to Vermont. We wrapped them carefully and stored them in the trunk of the BMW as we continued traveling south.

France's independence day, Bastille Day, July 14, was approaching. We decided to spend the holiday in the medieval town of Aigues-Mortes, down by the Mediterranean Sea on the western edge of the Camargue region. Being young and carefree, we made a sudden detour when we saw a sign in the direction of the city of Montpellier. As it turned out, our little hometown of Montpelier, Vermont, could not compare. France's Montpellier was a bustling city, boasting a population of nearly three hundred thousand, a large university, and a charming old-world commercial downtown neighborhood. We stopped by the city hall, and Gabrielle explained our special connection. Several local officials gathered and were pleasant and friendly as they queried about our little Montpelier. It took some effort to clarify that our capital city contained only seven thousand people and a small commercial downtown.

After this side trip, we then headed directly to Aigues-Mortes. It was an old, medieval, walled port city dating back to 1248. We did not have reservations, but Gabrielle quickly located a charming apartment flat near the downtown square. The impressive walls encompassing the small town were not only attractive, but they prevented automobile traffic. No cars were allowed entry, but a nearby field offered ample parking.

Our rental was an apartment in an old, charming house. The hosts were a hardworking young couple who spoke no English but provided a tastefully decorated room and delicious French-style home-cooked meals. This industrious couple prepared and served three meals daily, did all the house chores, managed the property, and even maintained an attractive flower garden.
Their charm and warmth quickly overcame communication difficulties, and their youthful vigor made me appreciate their effort to make us feel welcome and comfortable.

After settling in, we went to the outdoor dining area. As I savored my steak dinner on our first night, I agreed to accept a refill on another glass of delicious local red wine. Within a minute or two, the couple's young daughter, Camille, probably ten or eleven years of age, very carefully delivered the wine glass to our table. She walked with a natural grace and composure, and as she reached the table, a smile like a ray of sunshine unfolded. She spoke to me in French. And while I understood not a word, I was charmed. I smiled back. She had a sparkle in her eye and, even for a young child, a friendly, engaging personality. Gabrielle pointed to an empty seat at our table and, using sign language and some essential French words, invited Camille to join us after the meal was completed. She ended up sitting with us for the rest of the evening, smiling and making comments that were hard for me to comprehend. I could tell she enjoyed our company and attention.

We had advance notice that Aigues-Mortes had a unique festival on the eve of Bastille Day. When both proprietors spotted us sitting outside near their garden, they joined us. Gabrielle, using her best French, asked them about the upcoming celebration. They were animated with excited anticipation, but it was apparent that they were reluctant to leave their property. All five rooms in their guest house were occupied, and there was much to attend to. With that, they retreated to the kitchen.

As we sat outside in the little garden, Gabrielle turned to me and suggested we invite Camille to join us at the Bastille Eve celebration in the nearby town square. This was an unexpected but not unwelcome idea. After enjoying my first dinner at the pensione and two glasses of red wine, my mood was upbeat, and without hesitation, I concurred. Using some French, a little German, and some sign language, Gabrielle indicated our wishes to the parents, who quickly agreed, showering us with warm expressions of appreciation. As Camille followed the discussion, she leaped from her seat, jumped up and down, and hugged us.

Later the next afternoon, we collected our young charge as a crowd began to swell near the town center. French flags were on full display, augmented with large, attractive candles placed strategically around the large town square. We were greeted by a local group of musicians who played folk songs and patriotic marches. As the sunlight dimmed, townsfolk gathered in long lines held hands and danced and marched together with great joy. Although hesitant initially, Gabrielle, I, and our young companion, Camille, joined the procession. We were swept along, caught in this moving and romantic moment of simple pleasure in a community of strangers. The near-perfect evening ended with fireworks and a rousing rendition of La Marseillaise, the French national anthem.

We intended to get an early start the following day since we needed to be back in Darmstadt and prepare for a flight home in several days. As we sat down for breakfast, we were warmly greeted in the dining room, and like magic, warm croissants appeared along with fresh eggs and strong coffee. Anticipating our departure, we had loaded the car up the previous afternoon, but we still carried two backpacks.

We parted with hugs and kisses, remembering our stay and the celebration from the previous evening. Camille followed us as we approached one of the ten gated archways leading us outside the city walls and into the nearby parking area. As we turned the corner, we could see her silhouette with her arms waving with youthful enthusiasm and hopefully with good memories stored for future reflection.

Shock and dismay hit us like a blow to the stomach as we spotted our car. The beloved BMW had been ravaged and vandalized overnight. The sight was overwhelming. We surveyed the damage. Two back windows had been smashed, and a side-view mirror hung pathetically as the vandals had unsuccessfully tried to detach it. Besides our suitcase, several wrapped presents in a shopping bag were gone as were assorted shoes and sweaters left in the back seat. Most devastating was the absence of the vases that Gabrielle had so admired and valued. The loss was crushing. We felt violated and greatly regretted the disappointment that would soon hit her parents.

Perhaps this was a sad but not uncommon act of vandalism spurred by excessive drinking on a celebratory night. Yet our car was the only violated vehicle at least that we could discern. Several teenage boys passed, eyeing the carnage, and came over for a closer inspection. They spoke to us in English. One bold fellow pointed to our license plate, a German license plate, and indicated that German plates were a magnet for trouble. For a moment, I could not make sense of his commentary, but as I was to learn, the bitterness and hatred between France and Germany still lingered even though the Second World War ended more than forty-one years ago. I realized this as I confronted issues that were foreign to my comprehension. We never could prove the exact cause of the break-in, and no one was ever apprehended, but we suspected that the German license plates might indeed have been central to the attack.

Gabrielle and I were shaken. With a small crowd gathered, two young gendarmes wandered over and quickly assessed the damage. As if we were not confused and overwhelmed enough, they communicated to us in French, throwing in some basic English phrases that were less than helpful. After all, it was Bastille Day, a national holiday, and besides making a list of missing items, there was not much more to investigate.

As we stood by the car, I tried to cheer up Gabrielle, who was devastated. Of course, it was France's primary national holiday, and most of the country was on vacation. I asked her if she knew the French word for fingerprints, implying that the police in this little town might do well to rely on fingerprints to solve our crime. My attempt at humor fell flat. The police officers checked our passports and completed a short list of missing items. They had us start the car, and we were gratified when it roared to attention. Given the holiday, there was no chance of finding a mechanic. Locating an open gas station would be the best thing that could be expected.

We were both upset, overwhelmed not only with our loss but with the state of disrepair of the car. Our only thought was to get home. Gabrielle estimated that we could make it back to Darmstadt in six, maybe seven, hours. We found some cardboard padding to put across our front seats, covering glass splinters. Two local men, seeing our plight, offered some wire that Gabrielle used to tie down the back trunk although it was impossible to secure tightly without a working latch. Gabrielle was too unsettled and upset to drive, so I took the wheel and held it tightly for the entire trip.

We proceeded north, weaving through many charming villages adorned with Bastille Day decorations. After an hour of driving, we noticed the gas tank was getting low. Seeing a sign for an open gas station, Gabrielle directed me to an exit off the secondary highway we were driving on. I pulled in and tried to reassure Gabrielle that everything would be okay. Conflicting emotions tore me. I was trying to bolster Gabrielle's spirits while uncertain whether I could manage to drive all the way home.

An attendant came over to the car. He said something in French. I looked up at him with a blank look on my face. He was an intimidating, hulking fellow in his twenties. Gabrielle leaned over to my window and pointed to the desired gas for the old BMW. We were greeted with an uncomfortable, pregnant pause. The attendant barked some commands. Fortunately, Gabrielle quickly figured out what he was saying. He was asking for our car keys. The BMW was indeed an older model; he needed the ignition key to unlock the gas tank. I handed the key to the attendant, and as he retreated, I asked Gabrielle to go in and get me a large coffee as I anticipated the long ride ahead.

The attendant filled the tank, but when he headed back to the station, he seemed greatly agitated, and I heard him yelling at Gabrielle, who was stepping out of the station after securing a coffee from the vending machine. I got out of the car to see what was happening. Although I could not understand a word of his rant, I quickly understood that we faced a new, serious problem. Looking at his hand, I could only see half a key. It seems that when he opened the gas tank, he must have turned the key with unnecessary force because he was now fuming, screaming at us while holding only the top part of the ignition key, which had snapped in two.

Based on his animation and body language, the attendant seemingly was trying to blame us for the mishap. At that point, all three of us were in an uproar, and bad words were uttered, some in English, some in French, and some in German. Given what we had already been through that morning, I strained to control my emotions.

Gabrielle decided that it was time to call her father. We both dreaded the task but were at our wit's end. Using a pay phone inside the station, I wondered whether we needed a lawyer more than auto assistance. Pulling herself together, Gabrielle first detailed the robbery, then quickly described the damage to the car, ending with news of our latest disaster, the nonfunctioning half key. As far as I could discern, her father was calm and sympathetic, but he, too, was confused about how to proceed. Glumly, we sat in the station waiting for him to call us back with an update. Fifteen minutes later, he reported that he had found a second car key, but there was no way of promptly transporting it down to southern France. Besides, the forecast for the following day was for steady rain, which reinforced our need to get home.

As a last resort, we demanded that the attendant call the station owner at home. Reluctantly, he did so. Over the phone, Gabrielle conveyed the basic outline of our plight and distress. The station owner spoke reasonable English, which was a relief. His tone and manner seemed to calm Gabrielle, and she reported as she hung up that he was going to drive over to sort things out. He estimated that he could be over in fifteen minutes.

The owner, Andre, arrived a half hour later. He made an immediately favorable impression, apologizing while explaining that he had a whole house of company waiting to celebrate the holiday and needed to get them settled before heading to the station. His appearance quieted the young service attendant, who remained sullen but at least was no longer yelling at us. Surveying the scene, the owner first thought we were focused on assessing the car repairs that might be needed. Still, once we showed him the dysfunctional broken car key, he seemed to understand how upsetting our plight was.

He explained that the only solution to starting the car was to pull the wires out from inside the front dashboard and hot-wire the vehicle. He removed some of the front padding under the steering wheel using a small crowbar, and wires fell out in a tangle. He seemed to know what he was doing, and we were more than willing to follow his suggestion. Having wires hanging down by my lap was another upsetting intrusion. Within a couple of minutes, he instructed me to start the car. It turned over as I revved up the engine. This new solution further distorted the appearance of the car. For a fleeting moment, I found this disastrous scene—shattered windows, a trunk flipping up and down, and now wires hanging below the steering wheel and practically in my lap—hysterically funny.

We still had hours of driving ahead, and the owner clarified that we should not disengage the wires or let the car engine turn off. Any humorous thoughts were now displaced by fear and worry.

The station owner expressed dismay over our morning misadventures. However, he did not imply that the station was accountable for the broken key. He looked at us and the wrecked car, and in a moment of compassion, this stranger reached out to us with decency and kindness by inviting us to his nearby house for some refreshments before we headed north. Although Gabrielle was uncertain (she was so stressed that food seemed unappealing), I was appreciative and . . . hungry. Andre explained that they were about to start a barbecue lunch, and we could wash up, eat, and then head on our way; as he suggested, I followed his car and turned into his long driveway outside this French village.

Our misfortune had disrupted Andre's Bastille Day cookout, but in his absence, family members had already begun grilling some impressively large bratwurst with a keg of cold beer nearby. The family members, a dozen people of all ages, welcomed us warmly. While Gabrielle was still unsettled and lacking an appetite, I was a receptive and hungry guest. It was a sweet reprieve from an already stressful day, and the hospitality was appreciated. Given the trip ahead and how unsettled I felt, I drank only a Coke, leaving a beer fest for another occasion.

The BMW, with wires now disconnected, was the main attraction, and several family members offered various assessments and despair over the appearance of the family gem. Two teenage boys were particularly interested in the hot-wire arrangement, now sitting in a pile in the driver's seat.

After half an hour, Gabrielle and I offered heartfelt thanks and indicated we would depart for Germany. If nothing else, we had added some unexpected drama and excitement to Andre's holiday celebration. Reaching into the car, he reconnected the wires. I started the car and headed down the long driveway. In a typical American gesture, as I turned onto the main road, I lightly gave the horn a tap or two, and with a wave of my left arm, we departed.

The center of this little village was just a mile away, but I sensed that nothing would come easy on Bastille Day for us. Within a few seconds out on the main road, the horn again sounded without guidance from me. My reaction was to tap it, thinking that this would solve the problem. We entered the village center, and the square was busy with local folk celebrating their national holiday. As we circled the downtown square, residents started clapping and waving toward us, assuming, I guess, that our constant tooting of the horn was part of the Bastille Day festivities. The entangled wires on my lap were the culprit.

Dazed and confused, I agreed with Gabrielle's assessment that we retrace our steps and head back to Andres's house. With our horns blaring on and off, we drove up the long driveway and were momentarily greeted like long-lost friends. Andre disconnected the offending wires in less than three minutes, and silence reigned. We departed again to warm goodbyes, and I wonder to this day if several family members still mention our plight and visit on Bastille Day. As we drove down the driveway, I waved goodbye, extending my left arm, and told Gabrielle I would skip any attempt to toot the horn. A smile broke out for the first time that day, and she laughed heartily.

We did make it back to Darmstadt by nightfall with only one agitated moment. Two hours south of Darmstadt, we had to stop for gas. You can pump gas into a running car without blowing it up, an experiment I would prefer to experience only once in my life. The fear of turning off the ignition and then being unable to hot-wire the car made this a necessary experiment that day.

Gabrielle's father, a reserved but calm man, was a true soldier and gentleman. Upon our return, we both shuddered internally as he inspected the car. His face was grim. He made some witty remarks to Gabrielle although she never did translate his response for me. He expressed no anger or blame. Gabrielle's mother came over and hugged me and offered warm and compassionate words that Gabrielle translated.

Gabrielle's parents ushered us out to their backyard, and soon we were enjoying a fine bottle of wine and some delicious cold cuts, pickles, and a salad as the last hint of daylight faded. With improved spirits, we all agreed that there would be better days ahead for us and the family's BMW vintage motor car.

March Madness and Basketball

It was a major March blizzard in the early 1980s in Central Vermont. By midmorning, my young son Jamie had enjoyed his snow day by building a snowman. By noon, state workers were released, a rare event even now. When the legislative session got called off for the rest of the day, I knew we had a real nor'easter.

I watched the drama unfold on Sparrow Farm Road with an inner glee. Who doesn't relish the quiet beauty of mounting white piles on fields, back decks, and surrounding old barns? By early afternoon, the snow had spread like a blanket to the horizon.

In those days, we relied on WDEV radio out of Waterbury for weather reports, following their updates every hour. Naturally, I cranked up the wood stove—the heat offering comfort in an old farmhouse insulated with ancient copies of *Times Argus* newspapers stuffed into walls—and tuned my transistor radio to my favorite station. Their message was simple. Stay home.

The memory of this blizzard has dimmed, not unlike the view out back during a storm when the sight of stately white pine and balsam trees fades in and out with swirling snow. I am certain of one thing though. The storm happened on a Thursday.

Thursday evenings back then were marked on the calendar with a fervor known to religious zealots, complete with a sense of community, celebration, and tradition and amplified with familiar sights and sounds. The Montpelier Men's Basketball League games—sacred winter festivals at the Recreation Center on Barre Street, better known as our coliseum—were held on Thursday nights.

In reality, the basketball court fell short of regulation size, and the walls were too close to the playing area, but the court transformed middle-aged men into boys when the whistle sounded for the opening tip-off. This was true for both league games and the lunch-hour pickup encounters. For those who played, this little bandbox was our Madison Square Garden.

For the random collection of players representing all fields of endeavor—lawyers, loggers, teachers, construction workers, state employees, small business owners, and those in between jobs—going to the Rec Center for basketball games was our trip to Mecca. Scattered by the passing decades, these players craved not only the bright lights of the gym but the camaraderie and bonding known to central Vermont basketball warriors.

With the blizzard raging, only a fool would consider playing a league basketball game that evening. Nonetheless, at four in the afternoon, my loving partner turned to me and asked, "What are you doing, and where do you think you are going?" She was curious to know why I was zipping up my parka and laboring to put on heavy winter boots on my way out to shovel a path to my car, which slumped partly hidden under a mountain of fresh snow. This very action seemed strange even to me given that the storm was raging and a noticeable wind had also picked up. Why not wait until morning?

Even today, I am not sure there is a simple, absolute, rational explanation. Who can explain the attraction the enchanted Sirens had over Odysseus in Homer's epic tale?

Be that as it may, despite any rational behavior typical to a man in his mid-thirties, in the back of my somewhat distorted, if not disturbed, mind was the sacred mantra "the game must go on," a refrain instilled by coaches and adults from elementary school to high school and through college and beyond. If my actions were questionable, they were also spontaneous, activated by the tingling and tantalizing hope of enjoying the thrill of athletic battle, the joy of team camaraderie, the sight of graceful shots swishing through the hoop, and the pulsating tension of an uncertain outcome. I was well aware that the fraternity of central Vermont hoopsters shared this devotion to the game with a certain reckless enthusiasm.

Despite the blizzard, the cancellations near and far, and the enticing notion of staying by the wood stove, I shoveled around my car with a vigor that would have made John Henry proud. I took it as a sign from above, (and I am not a religious man) when after five-thirty, in the near-dark winter wonderland, I heard that distinct rumble of a snowplow coming down the road after a noted absence. That the plow created a new snow pile behind my car did not diminish my resolve. With the plow evident, the roads near my house were now visible although the snow continued unabated. Besides, my recent vigorous shoveling certainly served as a physical warm-up.

Just minutes after six, I returned to the house long enough to inhale a sandwich, grab a sports bag containing my lime-green Carriveau's Gulf gas station jersey, and bid farewell with a kiss, a hug, and a high five for Jamie. "You are crazy," said my partner Gabrielle with an emphasis on "crazy." She was wonderful in most ways but clearly deficient in understanding the Thursday night ritual. It probably never occurred to her that we were scheduled to play Julio's restaurant, the team that shared first place in league play.

At the top of Sparrow Farm Road, I turned onto North Street to that magnificent expanse with the Green Mountains totally exposed. The open vista invites wind and whiteouts. Vaguely, I saw the outline of the nearby Green Mountains, but there were swirling, blinding flakes screaming across the open field. There were two options: go back home or carry on. Using memory as a guide, I aimed forward in a straight line, hit the gas, and shot across the narrow road. I exhaled only when I reached a sheltered area protected by trees and shrubs.

Proceeding downhill on North Street is stimulating on a good day, and at specific points, one risks going over the guard rails and sliding downhill into the recreation complex or, with better luck, landing more softly on the baseball field. In a blinding snowstorm, the drive down that steep, curved hill is nothing short of heart-stopping. Gripping the wheel and applying the brake, I slowly wound down the steep decline. As I pulled into downtown Montpelier, I took comfort that traffic was exceptionally light. Who in their right mind would be out on a night like this?

Crawling slowly up snowbound Barre Street, I approached the gym. A magnificent sight greeted me: the gym lit up, illuminated by fresh snow and the many cars parked out front. As I carefully climbed snowy steps to the "cathedral entrance" and pulled open the heavy wooden door, I heard the distinct thumping of basketballs, the squeak of sneakers, and the banter of players as they warmed up.

Both teams had a full complement of players, true basketball warriors, that night. The game must go on—and it did—blizzard and rational behavior be damned!

The Bush Plane in Botswana

The bush plane sent to retrieve me from the wilds of interior Botswana circled for a second time. It then came down low, scattering a large herd of zebras, clearing the field momentarily below. The plane again tried to land but aborted the attempt after being buffeted and tossed about by ferocious winds blowing straight from the Kalahari Desert. I was relieved at this, for my stomach and heart were in a flutter. The thought of getting on that little one-propeller plane in these conditions terrified me, but I knew both my options and sense of control were limited. The diminutive plane disappeared, but, several minutes later, came back into view again. Then, shaking more like a windblown kite than a plane, and after some uneven, dramatic moments on its descent, it finally managed to reach the ground, rolling to a stop.

Years have passed but not the memory of this adventure. At that moment, I was gripped with fear—fear of flying and, frankly, fear of dying. Now, decades later, my terror has been replaced by more relaxed, even pleasant reflections, and from the present vantage point of my warm bed, the incident seems more amusing than frightening. Perhaps time really does help iron out wrinkles in life that seem deep and, in specific moments, horribly contorted.

The endless free time during our current pandemic winter seems to serve as an incubator for daydreaming sessions and imaginary videos of travels past. With nostalgic thoughts, I recall my trip to this special country in the south of Africa, and it causes me to remember many childhood associations with this distant continent. My youthful imaginings about Africa were very much linked to my reliance on the written word—not from old encyclopedias but from old ten-cent comic books that sadly, in retrospect, created my impressions not only of Africa but of racial and social stereotypes and more. We may not be prisoners of our past, but we are shaped and formed by it like rocks along an ancient, gushing river.

As I reflect on my first of several African journeys, I admit that it was none other than Tarzan who provided my first reference point. And as I traveled to Africa decades ago, with gleeful mirth, I casually compared my own coping abilities to those displayed in Tarzan's brave and heroic feats as recorded in countless comic books and movies. I conclude, in the warmth of my bed, that even the great warrior himself would have been challenged by the antics of that swaying bush plane as it traversed the wilds of an expansive game preserve in Botswana.

In 2004, I was invited to travel to South Africa to work with mental health leaders in that vibrant, complex, and expansive country. My key contact was an energetic, charismatic, and resourceful woman, a white expatriate from England named Zane Wilson. By coincidence and luck, Zane and I had attended the same conference in DC a year earlier. After hearing me address the forum, she insisted that I reserve time to travel to South Africa to work with her so that I could serve as a mental health consultant to and for community groups, service organizations, practitioners, insurance administrators, and elected officials.

Zane was insistent, persuasive, clever, and truly a "force of nature" who directed one of that country's largest mental health organizations. Her resources to underwrite my trip might have been limited but not her creativity or her enthusiasm. Trying to entice me, she offered to purchase a first-class ticket on the nearly nineteen-hour nonstop flight from New York to Johannesburg, but I begged off. It seemed too privileged for my taste and too extravagantly expensive given my frugal nature. Not to be deterred, in turn, using her boundless contacts in Africa and her penchant to barter with friends, colleagues, and business contacts, she arranged for me to have a four-day safari in the wilds of Botswana, adding extra time to my now more than three-week work assignment. I found this to be a much-preferred barter arrangement, more appealing for sure than a first-class airplane seat.

On my first morning in Johannesburg, I met with mental health leaders and elected officials at a welcoming breakfast meeting. However, the occasion was marred by an elevator mishap, which caused some drama when I was caught between floors in a malfunctioning lift. I arrived late for the meeting, dirty, and disheveled. This rousing, nearly disastrous, beginning reminded me that you only get one chance to make a first impression.

After this session, I was introduced to Thabo, an older native who assisted Zane's organization as a driver. His English was better than my Zulu; Zulu was his African tribe. I had packed my bag, and as planned, we set out by car for Botswana, a journey of more than five hours. Before long, I learned about his youthful days growing up and living during the apartheid years followed by the euphoria and freedom associated with the election, in 1994, of Nelson Mandela to the nation's highest position.

Thabo was an engaging and enthused storyteller, but his skills were not as advanced when it came to driving and following directions. He tended to speed up as we approached narrow rural roads, and in towns, he sometimes missed or ignored red lights. As we approached the five-hour mark, it was apparent that we were horribly lost, and as it turned out, we ended up bypassing the official border crossing. Desperate for help, Thabo stopped at a lonely dwelling on a deserted road. Here a woman, speaking in Zulu, informed him about our present location in Botswana and hinted at some generalized directions to the hidden gem of the Madikwe Game Reserve where I was booked for four days.

It took a while, but we finally found and drove to the entrance of the safari reserve. I checked in with the game reserve rangers, a rugged and sturdy-looking crew who looked ready for any adventure out in the bush country. I was relieved and pleased when they found my reservation and assigned me to small, quaint, rustic shelter, more of a hut than a formal dwelling. It consisted of two cozy rooms as well as a most tiny toilet augmented by an enormous outdoor bathtub that some white colonial ruler might have left behind. Before heading off, the ranger demanded that I not walk around our encampment unless accompanied by an armed staff member. He alluded to "the tragedy" of the previous year but failed to offer specifics. Although I thought about asking whether a guest eaten by a lion was entitled to a full or partial refund, restraint seemed a better option, a strategy that was not always my strength.

From Thursday until midafternoon the following Monday, I was a euphoric captive to one of life's great travel experiences. Each morning, a knock on my door at five A.M. signaled the beginning of a safari adventure. With a small crowd of other tourists, I climbed into an open safari vehicle with a driver and tracker up front. We set off each cool morning before sunrise after a strong coffee and delicious African cakes, heading out to a world of wonder. As daylight ensued, we sat expectantly by various watering holes and silently watched herds of zebras, hippos, African buffalo, impalas, wildebeest, leopards, and huge black rhinoceroses gather. Without fail, we were rewarded with groups or a tribe of elephants trumpeting as they made their way into this fantastic wildlife scene, magnificent in their size and power. Giraffes were also abundant throughout the reserve, and to further enrich each drive, we saw countless birds and amazing flora of every description. Later each day, before sunset, there was another daily game drive.

It was during the later safari that we came upon several impressive and aristocratic-looking lions. On the afternoon trip, we watched transfixed as two lions stalked their prey. We watched them for nearly an hour as they killed and feasted on the remains of a springbok antelope. An evening later, we again experienced the eternal struggle between life and death in this natural environment as a pack of hyenas attacked and ultimately killed a young cape buffalo.

My dwelling was now like a second home, graced with a rather romantic sleeping net enclosing my bed. A small but welcoming overhead fan provided cooling relief from the intense African heat. However, I had to remember to duck carefully when passing since a beheading would ruin the day.

On Sunday morning, upon our return from our early excursion and following a hearty breakfast, I decided to luxuriate in the large outdoor bathtub near my comfortable dwelling. Cheered on by a glorious sun and aided by some thick foliage that shielded me from my nearest safari neighbors, I went outside, stripped off my clothes, dropped them in a heap, and climbed into the beckoning tub. This was a moment of pure, unadulterated bliss. Besides the scenery and African ambiance, being able to stretch out completely in an oversize bath is a rare and joyous occasion when one is well over six feet tall.

After soaking for ten minutes or so, I sensed a stirring in the surrounding brush that encircled my tub. To my amazement, two fearsome-looking baboons appeared. They stood there, some thirty feet away, looking at me with uncertain intent. I watched them. They watched me. Much to my surprise ("shock" might be more accurate), within a minute or two, at least forty or fifty baboons silently slid from the surrounding underbrush and gathered in an arc around my bathtub. Several of them started making guttural noises while many of the young primates seemed animated or perhaps agitated by the scene. The troop slowly encircled me. As they did, I felt increasingly uneasy, vulnerable, alone, and out of my element. Relying on basic instinct and propelled by a growing sense of danger, perhaps panic, I extricated myself from the tub, rushed over to pick up my clothes, and bolted naked in full retreat toward my lodging. With the quick speed of an old athlete, I made it to the hut, rushed in, and slammed the door shut, using the bolt for added protection. There I was, the not so great or brave "white hunter," peering through the curtains, naked as a jaybird, and checking—once again—to make sure the door was indeed tightly latched. Within a minute or two after my impulsive, unsightly performance, the baboons quietly disappeared as they slid back into the bush after what may have been an entertaining morning for them. It occurred to me that Tarzan might not have approved my fearful and timid reaction that left me vulnerable, especially without weapons or clothes.

The following day was to be my last in this paradise. The plan called for Thabo to drive over early in the morning and then escort me back to Johannesburg in time for my participation in an evening radio interview based in the city. I awoke early that day and knew immediately that there was a serious weather episode developing outside. While the morning stars suggested clear skies, a ferocious wind was stirring, bending, and swaying the surrounding palm trees most dramatically. Sipping coffee in the dark before departing for the morning safari trip, our guides informed us as we climbed aboard vehicles that this was a significant windstorm by way of the not-too-distant Kalahari Desert.

Upon our return that morning, I was summoned to the head ranger's office. Waiting for me was a message from Zane indicating that Thabo had major car problems and would not be able to make the drive to Botswana. This news update came over a telex machine housed in the dining room that seemed rather quaint, something like a scene out of an old movie. Within minutes, I rationalized that perhaps this turn of events was for the best. I could wait another day to begin work, and Zane might be willing to do the radio show without me that evening. With luck, I might even be able to take another safari drive.

It was with relief that I sat down for a splendid brunch, and as I finished my second cup of coffee, the head ranger once again approached my tablemates and me and provided further news. To my amazement, he informed me that Zane Wilson, ever resourceful and determined, had hired a bush pilot from Johannesburg to fetch me at around four in the afternoon, which would enable me to participate in the scheduled evening radio show highlighting mental health services in South Africa. Reaction to the news was mixed. My new friends seemed genuinely concerned for my safety. Outside, the winds roared. Inside the dining room, several safari travelers openly worried about flying in this turbulent weather.

Although I came to South Africa alone, by chance, there was a small group of evangelical born-again Christians on safari when I was at the reserve. This Alabama-based group sponsored a project in South Africa and decided to take a side trip to Botswana as well. They were pleasant except that several of them had a tendency to proselytize their religious beliefs. This occurred as we ate meals and even, on occasion, during long safari drives together. I could not help but think about my long-departed grandfather who was a strict old-world Orthodox Jew with little or no contact with people outside the faith. I wondered whether he was listening to these conversations. If so, I was certain he was turning over in his grave.

I did the best I could, but this was not an easy fit. We were strange bedfellows, all of us many miles from home. In response and possibly to give my newfound friends some grief, I focused much of my conversation on Howard Dean, presidential candidate Dean, that energized liberal from Vermont who clearly was not at all a favorite of the evangelical crowd. Despite our differences, the sharing of the magnificent early morning safari excursions helped to foster a feeling of camaraderie.

Knowing of my pending flight back to Johannesburg, we sat together inside, escaping the winds and occasional blasts of sand. To my surprise, these zealous evangelicals rose, encircled my chair, and began a spirited and fervent prayer session to promote and ensure my safe travels. They called on Jesus himself to protect me from the dangers ahead and to continue my efforts to improve mental health services in South Africa. With a final benediction, the group held hands, grasped mine, and pulled me into their circle. Despite my reservations and opposition to the evangelical movement, I offered warm thanks, and I admit, in this case, I meant it.

In the middle of the afternoon, a young ranger picked me up and drove us some ten bumpy miles in the game reserve to an area that was referred to as the "landing zone." While I could agree that the general area was more open than other forest-like and densely tree-covered terrain, I detected nothing that would suggest a landing strip. What I did notice were several herds of large animals grazing along the imaginary airstrip and runway.

With no sign of the plane, my spirits soared as I considered the virtue of having one more day on the safari adventure. My relaxed mood changed when I heard the slight drone of a small aircraft and then I spied an unimpressive small plane with its one propeller in full motion. It flew low, and it was bruised and dented. Although the pilot's first two attempts to land were aborted in the windstorm, I noticed that he skillfully managed to fly low in a way that cleared the wildlife from a possible landing area. This fellow knew how to fly a bush plane and shepherd the beasts below. To my chagrin, his third attempt at landing was successful.

The pilot was a cocky but appealing young white man born somewhere in Mozambique. What he may have lacked in experience, he made up in reckless, somewhat good-natured, self-assurance. Of course, I was the only passenger, so he helped me climb into the plane. Given my height and the plane's low ceiling, it was more of a crawl though. He pointed to the one battered and not very tightly secured seat behind his and suggested that, given the look on my pallid face, I help myself to a beer or two from his cooler, which was sitting on the floor as if we were on our way to a picnic lunch. Not waiting on formality, I reached for a semi-warm Castle Lager and took some refreshment with the hope that it would calm my nerves. Sensing my fear, worry, and ambivalence, this young daredevil tried to reassure me by announcing that should we crash near takeoff, we would both probably be eaten by lions before nightfall. He roared with laughter.

With that cheerful comment, he gunned the engine and we took off. Animals below darted this way and that as the little propeller lifted us aloft. At first, the winds tossed us roughly, and the plane dipped and dodged, leaving me with doubt about getting on board. An image appeared in my mind of a copy of our local newspaper with a headline story, "Local man devoured by lions in the jungle - no refund offered."

As we headed south, however, the turmoil abated, and we pointed in the direction of Johannesburg. Peering out the little window—more of a slit than a window—I gazed below at the unfamiliar terrain, and tried to imagine the adventures and challenges that awaited me during my three weeks of work. Before I'd departed for Botswana, Zane had provided a paper outlining some of my upcoming activities including a fifteen-minute interview on *Morning Live South Africa* television news show, a meeting with political leaders in Pretoria, a presentation at Cape Town University, and a consultation with representatives of the country's insurance industry.

I had confidence in my ability to handle these assignments, but still, it sent chills up my spine as we began our now tranquil descent into South Africa's largest city. As we landed, I felt relief and excited anticipation. Having survived my adventures in Botswana, I was ready to tackle this amazing assignment.

I Remember Mama

"I don't want my son to be a freak."

That was my mother's lament. No one would accuse my mom of being timid about voicing and expressing her concerns. It wasn't just the words, mind you, but the excessive volume and the spoken tone of desperation about this perceived crisis. Perhaps it was her way of showing motherly love. Still, her presentation certainly lacked a tad of compassion and awareness, not to mention some insight into the fragile nature of adolescent development.

These words still resonate, although they were spoken more than six decades ago as we sat huddled in the small examination room of my doctor's office. I can still recall and remember my sense of embarrassment and adolescent confusion. Having just turned thirteen years of age, I had already experienced an early growth spurt. To add to my teenage angst, some older classmates had recently started calling me "tiny" not with affection but with derision. I was taller by far than most of my contemporaries although skinny as a rail. As a young adolescent, I was not blessed with a great self-image.

"I don't want my son to be a freak," she repeated a second time with more urgency and despair as the doctor entered the cubicle. My mother had dragged me to this appointment because she carried the hope that something could be done to slow my growth. This seemed strange, but I had no say or control.

Dr. Reynolds, our family physician, had a kind demeanor, graying hair, and a dry sense of humor. It wasn't that long ago, when I was younger, ailing from the flu or some illness, that he had made several house visits accompanied by an impressive, sizable black doctor's bag. But today, as we said hello, the doctor clasped my hand in his and expressed his sympathy over the recent death of my father just three months earlier. Since my mother hardly ever discussed or mentioned this life-changing event with me or anyone else, I found comfort in his words and caring gestures.

The doctor proceeded with a cursory examination, telling my mother she was welcome to sit in as he carefully measured my height. "Just a shade over six foot three inches," he reported. He felt my bones, then consulted a sizable medical book on a shelf near his desk. Much to my chagrin, he asked me my shoe size. In a low voice, I mumbled my reply, and he wrote on his information sheet the number thirteen. He then turned to my mother and, with a slightly mischievous smile, asked, "Do you have any members of your immediate family who are seven-footers? Maybe Ken will be a basketball player.".

I laughed, but my mother's face was contorted with worry. "Can't you do anything?" she wailed.

Dr. Reynolds was kind but firm in his response. "Mrs. Libertoff, you are fortunate to have a healthy son who will probably be tall—tall and handsome," he added.

We departed his office with few other words. My mother retreated into silence on the drive back home. I was relieved that this appointment was over.

The following day, my mother announced that we were going shopping. Clothes shopping was not on my priority list, and going with my mother was not something I looked forward to. In fact, it set off alarm bells and blinking red lights like some advanced nuclear warning system. Based on experience, I knew that my mom was a bold, aggressive, and, frankly, impolite shopper, especially when she had her eye on some "must-have" outfit for herself. And my mother was loud, loud enough to attract attention. I had been mortified when a department store salesperson told her to "tone it down" the last time she dragged me along as she shopped for clothes. Adding insult to injury, she and another woman had fought over a bargain bin filled with spring outfits while I hid at some distance, embarrassed and self-conscious.

Worst of all, my mother was overbearing when buying me clothes, especially pants. For reasons that remain a mystery to me, she seemed obsessed with ensuring plenty of room in the crotch area. Without fail, she would express this concern, in her loud and piercing New York City voice, to me, the salespeople, and anyone else within shouting distance. Talk about public shaming.

The following day, as we departed, my mother was somber and quiet. I was already aware of her many moods, so I dutifully got in the car without protest or question. We drove in silence to neighboring Brooklyn just over the bridge. Mom had a terrible sense of direction and was a distracted driver, so it was a miracle that we found the street and parking lot of the unfamiliar store that was our intended destination.

Above the main door in enormous letters was a large sign, The Big Man's Shop, followed by roman numeral letters XXL. Although I was confused by this XXL stuff, I could tell from the size of the mannequins in the window that I was in for a new shopping experience. Our recent visit to the doctor did have some immediate repercussions, and my mother was a woman who was motivated to act on her fears and worries.

When we stopped at the front counter, the salesperson inquired about our specific needs. Using her forceful and mother-knows-best voice, Mom indicated that I needed some new pants and shirts, adding with diplomatic flair, "Something he can grow into." Through the intercom, a call went out to men I will refer to as Ron and Steven, who—we were assured—were knowledgeable, veteran salespeople at the shop and supposedly skilled in assisting teenagers.

Ron was indeed a big man. I would have guessed that he weighed more than three hundred pounds. Being a big fan of professional wrestling, I had some expertise on the size and girth of heroes like Killer Kowalski and Gorilla Monsoon, who were also in the three hundred-pound range. Ron, however, was much shorter than either of my favorites and was egg-shaped and flabby rather than muscular and athletic. Before saying a word, we were joined by one of the tallest men I had ever seen in person—at least to that point in my life. Steven was elevated, but unfortunately, he had a noticeable slouch in his posture and might be referred to as an ungainly giant. As they stood by my side together, Ron and Steven made me look . . . for lack of a better word, tiny and, if not tiny, then simply small and ordinary.

I could tell from my mother's face that she was flabbergasted at the girth and the size of these men. Later, when we were alone, she would refer to them as freaks. Since my mother was a woman of "strong opinion" and was, at times, unmercifully critical of others, particularly others that didn't match up to her standards of conformity, her harsh commentary did not strike me as unusual.

My mother was certainly not perfect, but to her credit, she was a force of nature at times, and indeed, when she was out shopping, she was determined not to be denied. Ron and Steven presented several pairs of dress slacks along with several shirts as she had requested, although both men expressed doubt from the start that these rather large garments would fit my slender, skinny frame.

They guessed correctly. I tried one of the shirts in the dressing room and then came out for review. To my amazement, the sleeve covered most of my hand, and although this was the smallest size they carried, the shirt made it look like I was wearing a parachute. Putting the shirts aside, mom ordered me back to the dressing room to try on pants. They were so roomy in the waist that I had to hold on to the seams as I walked out for fear of them falling. My mother's eyes narrowed, and for the first time I could ever remember on a shopping trip, my mother didn't even bother to ask in her loud, amplified voice whether there was ample room for growth.

To my surprise, when we departed The Big Man's Shop, absent a box or bag of purchases, my mother suggested that we go out for lunch at a nearby ice cream parlor. I was aware that my mother was prone to significant mood swings. Innocent as I was at thirteen, I later understood that these mood swings would escalate into powerful signals of deep-rooted mental illness. Agitated and despairing as she had been at the doctor's office the day before and as solemn as she had been when we headed to Brooklyn in the morning, she now seemed gay, almost euphoric. Going to The Big Man's Shop was therapeutic, and perhaps it put her concerns about me and my future growth and height in a better perspective. With no restraint, she laughed as she regaled me and total strangers seated at several nearby tables about the size and girth of the two salespeople, calling them better suited to the circus than their current occupation. She referred to Ron as a fat slob and added some offensive commentary while describing Steven as an ungainly giraffe.

Mom was such a complex person. At times, she could show great empathy. Yet this same person could be mean and cutting. She possessed a sharp tongue, and when so moved, she could mercilessly mow people down as if swinging a scythe in a flower garden. Being young and wanting to please, like a conspirator who only wanted to share her better mood, I laughed and probably egged her on.

I never grew to seven feet tall and never bought any clothes from The Big Man's Shop, but I will always remember sharing a delicious black-and-white ice cream soda that day. She wasn't perfect, but she was and always will be my one-of-a-kind mother.

Small World Connections

"*D*id I overhear you say *real maple syrup?*"
We looked up from our empty plates. Just fifteen minutes or so ago, our breakfast feast was stacked high. In response to the question, we nodded affirmatively and engaged our weary, sleepy-eyed, middle-aged waitress in what became a surprisingly meaningful and heartfelt conversation.

In November of 2021, we arrived in New Mexico at the start of an adventurous twelve days in the great Southwest. Following a long day of air travel from Burlington to Albuquerque, I was ready for an early, hearty breakfast. I am a good eater, and there is nothing wrong with basic diner fare back home, but now I anticipated a special southwestern meal. I am a devoted fan of spicy Mexican food, like huevos rancheros prepared with red and green chili, which warms my heart and palate.

Traveling is a favorite activity, and our recent trip combined family visits to New Mexico and Arizona while also touring such diverse places as Santa Fe, Sedona, the old hilltop mining town of Jerome, and the desert-like environment of Lake Havasu near the California border. It has always struck me that when traveling, one learns a lot about . . . oneself, not to mention one's traveling companions. Drafting plans in advance is helpful for us; the anticipation of an adventure fuels the spirit and soul. But there are usually some differences about priorities, levels of comfort, and, of course, the costs associated with leaving home. Finding a compromise is not always easy.

I am inclined to seek out simple, frugal accommodations while my wife, Sarah, seems to enjoy the thrill of an overpriced room in a more upscale hotel that is spotless and in perfect order. Besides not wanting to waste money, I prefer rubbing shoulders with the grittier aspects of life on the road where one meets *real people* as opposed to plastic, dull robots who often are bland and end a conversation with wishes for a good day without looking up from their fancy hotel front desk computer screen.

To balance our differences, on this trip, we took turns selecting sleeping quarters. I had the first choice, which is how we ended up at the San Mateo Inn in Albuquerque. Even I had to laugh with muted amusement at the brilliance of naming this facility an inn since, even to the uneducated eye, the facility was an old, shabby, and run-down motel that had seen better days. But who is to quibble when the daily rate is $69?

Our room presented us with some issues and challenges. The central light fixture near the beds did not work, and the front desk folks admitted that it needed attention. After a day and a half of a rather gloomy, dark atmosphere, this malfunction was corrected although several attempts failed, making us wonder why they gave us this room to begin with. Sarah again exposed her lofty standards when reporting that the rug in our room was unsatisfactory, claiming it was sticky. Thinking positively, I suggested that perhaps the inn applied some unique formula to keep older patrons from tripping and falling.

It might have been the inn's commitment to frugality and keeping things basic that found our abode lacking stoppers in both the bathroom sink and bathtub. And after a brief search, we agreed that the room did not come with every amenity . . . like a box of tissues. My suggestion to substitute toilet paper for tissues did not go over well. Although I didn't dare to comment, I did detect a specific odd stale odor that permeated our little love nest.

When we engaged with staff at the front desk, they were, however, extremely sympathetic, warm with concern, and generally caring, even if they struggled to solve most problems. Sarah, despite her reservations about the place, gave them high marks for "trying" and for being "engaged." We learned much about the life history of several front desk staff who shared details about growing up in the Land of Enchantment, identifying local hotspots and providing recommendations for cheap food. They pointed out one tangible asset of staying at the inn, namely its proximity to a nearby Denny's restaurant that was steps away.

For the first three mornings, we walked out of the front door of the San Mateo and practically landed at the front door of Denny's restaurant. While the beautiful Sandia Mountains loom tall over the city, our view from the inn was limited to the back of the restaurant, which, while not inspiring, let us know when the vast garbage bins in the back needed attention. I was uplifted, however, to learn from the front desk staff that our San Mateo key afforded us a ten percent discount on meals at Denny's, causing me to take comfort that we were saving even more money.

We both wanted a stack of pancakes, but to get the pancakes at this local Denny's, you had to order the Grand Slam, an "All American" meal that indeed was a colossal hit. Our waitress rattled off the deal, which, of course, started with two great and handsome pancakes accompanied by two eggs, two pieces of bacon, two pieces of sausage, a helping of potatoes, and, finally, two buttered pieces of toast. As a bona fide "good eater," I had little to complain about—*except* that I refuse to eat pancakes with fake syrup, which usually comes in a large plastic container with no identifying labels. While my culinary standards are low, I refuse to eat this breakfast treat without good old *Vermont maple syrup*.

Being a loyal and patriotic Vermonter, I always carry a small container of maple syrup purchased at Morse Farm up on Country Road outside Montpelier when I anticipate a pancake restaurant treat away from home. After making derogatory remarks about the fake stuff, I produced my cherished Morse Farm container. What joy and what pleasure to slyly open my liquid gold and smother our pancakes with the *real thing*. Even Sarah, who years ago found my behavior to be "unusual," had to agree that my approach had some virtue. As I took pains to remind her, it was a sound economic strategy with hints of frugality since many restaurants, especially high-end restaurants, provide real maple syrup but only when adding an extra exorbitant fee to the bill.

With a stack of beautiful pancakes all buttered up, I fumbled in my jacket pocket and pulled out my attractive glass container from Morse Farm and poured the syrup with anticipatory glee. And for that moment, the shortcomings at the inn melted as Sarah, too, worked her way through the stacked pancakes enhanced and graced by amber-colored Vermont syrup.

"Did I overhear you say real maple syrup?" our waitress asked as she slipped our bill on the table. This stranger, this hardworking, decent woman who looked like she had been serving food since before sunrise that morning, came closer to inspect the attractive syrup bottle shaped like a maple leaf.

To our surprise, as we looked at her, tears welled in her eyes, and she momentarily could not talk, overcome with emotion. This stranger with wet cheeks suddenly transformed before us in this unexpected intimate moment. Dabbing her eyes dry, she collected herself and related in a halting, strained voice how her dear, deceased mother always glazed the family Thanksgiving turkey with great Vermont maple syrup. The recipe was now part of her holiday tradition. She fondly told us how her mom splurged over this special Thanksgiving treat, hinting at modest family means. Seeing our maple syrup bottle obviously triggered a chain reaction of emotions that keyed into her affection for her mother and nostalgia for family Thanksgiving gatherings during her younger years.

As she composed herself, all three of us were moved. We thanked her for sharing this slice of her family history. Inspired by her story, we suggested that when we prepare our Thanksgiving turkey later in November, we also coat it with a dollop of maple syrup in honor of her mom.

We paid our bill and headed out. Thanks to the San Mateo Inn and the nearby Denny's, our chance encounter in New Mexico reaffirmed the goodness and shared humanity that can flow from connections with total strangers, giving hope for family memories and the future.

Memories and Life Lessons with Rodrigo

With time on my hands and activity centered around the old homestead, life during the pandemic caused some strange behaviors. For example, one late March day in 2021, I felt a sudden surge of energy and a dose of manly courage. With resolve, I made my way down the creaky stairs to the basement and located several huge bins filled with stuff.

Calling it "stuff" does not do it justice. These containers are a partial, if a disorganized, record of my life, snapshots capturing meaningful past experiences, an unscripted mosaic of items—filled with news clippings, countless photographs, old letters, and mementos.

Hauling up just one large bin was more challenging than I remember. It seemed heavier and bulkier than when I carried it down to an open spot in the cellar a couple of decades ago. Returning to my office, I carefully opened the container lid. Immediately, a couple of items fell out of the overstuffed box.

Grabbing an assortment of papers near the top, I found a treasure trove of clippings and countless news articles related to my three decades of work at the Vermont Association for Mental Health.

With relish, I read old but familiar news accounts reporting on numerous advocacy campaigns that culminated in the passage of laws like Vermont's parity bill in 1997. This legislation, entitled An Act Relating to Health Insurance for Mental Health and Substance Abuse, became the nation's most comprehensive parity law, mandating equality of health insurance for mental health and substance abuse conditions. Another achievement was the successful campaign to limit the influence and reach of the pharmaceutical industry in Vermont. This legislation, the Vermont Prescribed Products Gift Ban and Disclosure law, was recognized as a new national standard when it passed in 2009.

Sifting through the clippings, I pulled out a detailed news account of the successful campaign to end the practice of shackling Vermont teenagers in state custody whenever they needed transportation including visits to a doctor's office or to counseling sessions. Next, I glanced at an old article from *USA Today*, which reported on a major controversy related to the Vermont Teddy Bear Company's disregard for the stigmatization of mental illness when they promoted "Crazy for You" bears complete with a straitjacket and commitment papers.

Rummaging through the bin, I found many newspaper accounts of high school and college basketball games . . . some with pictures. Can that be me, number 44, leaping high as if I had helium in my sneakers in an account from a Far Rockaway High School game against rival Franklin K. Lane High in 1960?

My concentration on the image was so intense that I almost failed to notice this photo had a somewhat discolored tinge around the sides, reminding me of old textbook Civil War pictures. I came across another old picture taken four years later. There I was, wearing number 34 for the UConn Huskies in college, defending against players from Duke University in a tournament game, young and vigorous.

Reviewing the varied items, I opened a packet of old love letters tied together with a large rubber band. I suddenly experienced an extra heartbeat as I read several old but still legible letters sent by mail in days of old. These letters brought back the palpitations I associated with mail delivery six or seven decades ago—that delicious moment of anticipation just before opening a sealed note. Several of the texts were quite legible, with messages of affection and love. The intimacy and intensity contained in this correspondence seem much more impactful compared to today's terse emails and text messages.

Although I intended to cull through the voluminous items fueled by a desire to sort and organize this mess, when I finished my first run-through, I had only seven or eight items that might contribute to my next woodstove fire. It turns out that most of these gems are a representative snapshot of my life, and who knows, I might need to refer to some past legislative story or recall a tense basketball game in the 1950s or '60s, or even track down my senior year high-school heartthrob to check and see if she still can do the resounding Rockaway High cheer ending in an acrobatic tumble.

As I returned most of these treasures back into the bin, I retrieved two items that were priceless gems.

The first was an envelope with an enclosed letter from *Sports Illustrated* magazine dated some three decades ago. I laughed out loud—an infrequent experience during the pandemic's early weeks—and read the enclosed letter. The enlarged cursive lettering was addressed not to me but to Marina Libertoff. The letter offered Marina a special subscription offer. A ten-dollar payment ensured that she would receive a first-class mailing of a large wall calendar featuring models from the last *Sports Illustrated* annual swimsuit edition. I couldn't help but laugh.

There is more to the story. A week later, the phone rang, and the *Sports Illustrated* subscription office was on the line wanting to talk directly to Marina Libertoff about the recent solicitation. With a calm, matter-of-fact tone, I paused before responding and replied, "She can't come to the phone right now. Marina is out in the back field."

You see, Marina was a splendid Norwegian Fjord horse who was part of my family for some years when I was involved and in love with a woman named Gail. Although I was initially skeptical, not about the relationship but about having a four-legged pet of considerable size and girth, I came to love this handsome horse. In a moment of reckless abandon years ago, in honor of my devotion, I put my *Sports Illustrated* magazine subscription in Marina's name. At least I did not lie to the caller from the *Sports Illustrated* staff. Marina was busy out back!

The second gem that I retrieved was a photo of my grandson Rodrigo. I remember this picture as if it were yesterday. It captures a moment in time when we were together in New York City when he was nine or ten years of age. He was already a little "mensch," all big eyes and big heart, and at an age when exploring New York was exciting if a little overwhelming. The photo shows Rodrigo on a Manhattan Street, and he seems to be standing next to . . . a life-sized bowling pin or perhaps a big person inside a giant bowling pin costume. If it sounds like more information is needed, you are right.

Let me start by saying that I have two grandchildren who flew out of the sky and into my heart in 2007. I am not making this up. My son Jamie married Frida, a woman from Peru who came to Boston to seek a better life and to send money home to help support her two young children in Lima. After the marriage, there was an expectation that the children would come to the United States. However, plans were foiled and significantly delayed after the 9/11 tragedy, which greatly restricted and even closed access to our borders. Although circumstances delayed their travels to America, the children—Fiorella, the older sister of fourteen, and Rodrigo, younger at six—eventually got permission to leave. They flew together from Lima, Peru, to their new home in Albuquerque, New Mexico. This adventure was an odyssey: two kids traveling alone, entering a new country with a new family, a new language, a new culture, new schools, a new stepfather, and even a new grandfather somewhere in the wilds of New England.

Weeks after their arrival, I made my way to New Mexico and embraced my new grandkids. Even at age fifteen, Fiorella was a confident teenager, short in stature but with striking Peruvian features. She spoke English as a second language but was far from comfortable with her comprehension. Entering Sandia High School in Albuquerque as a new student, she was motivated to do well, but that first term was not easy. She was an intelligent young woman with a mind of her own. I remember her telling me how immature and lacking American boys seemed. She made a terrible mistake—now forgiven—when she mentioned that several boys from the Sandia High School basketball team were in her class. I think to show off her expanding English vocabulary, she said something about these young athletes being . . . dumbbells. Her commentary seemed overly harsh, even if somewhat accurate, given my devotion to athletic endeavors and basketball in particular.

Little Rodrigo radiated both warmth and an engaging shyness. Even at his young age and new to life in America, he exhibited an endearing kindness and sweetness. On the day I first met him, we stood next to each other in Jamie's kitchen and gazed at each other, mute but with radiating hearts. Rodrigo spoke not one word of English, and my Spanish was rudimentary at best.

Looking up at me with his big brown eyes making contact, he mumbled some words incomprehensible to me. Still, I could decipher some distant relationship with the English language as he recited from memory the following in the most unknown of dialects: "Way back, way back, it's a home run over Green Monster; the Red Sox win; the Red Sox win!" The inspiration for this incredible verbal presentation was found in my son's kitchen drawer. As a present to Jamie the previous year, I had gifted him a bottle opener that when activated, played a message about the victorious Red Sox baseball team. Rodrigo was fascinated by this device, which became a special toy and would also serve as his introduction to the English language. Who needs remedial language classes when you have a Red Sox bottle opener that talks to you?

By the time the photo with Rodrigo and the human bowling

pin was snapped, nearly four years had passed, and he was considerably more fluent in English. It amazed me how quickly he acclimated and assimilated to life in New Mexico. He visited Vermont every summer and bonded with my partner, Sarah, now my wife. She noticed that one challenge Rodrigo had was understanding American slang and idioms like "There is no such thing as a free lunch," or "A penny saved is a penny earned." She proved an able educator, plying him with idioms common to those of us growing up in the States.

His visit during the summer of his tenth year was particularly memorable. Rodrigo fell in love with Vermont during his earlier summer visits, but as a special treat, I decided that he and I would take a trip down to New York to visit my mother in Manhattan. It was exciting to arrive at Penn Station by train and catch a public bus down to Greenwich Village where my mom had an apartment.

Rodrigo already knew that his Grandpa Ken was a frugal man. "A penny saved is a penny earned," I reminded Rodrigo as we waited in the summer city heat and climbed onto the local bus going downtown. It was a hot, sticky day, and we noticed immediately that although the cooling system made considerable noise, it produced no refreshing air. Rodrigo did not seem convinced about the virtues of New York City's bus system as he wiped his sweaty brow. Still, he understood the rationale for taking public transportation rather than a much more expensive private cab. My grandson was developing a keen sense of humor, and he mentioned, with a mischievous grin, that maybe next time we could walk all the way and save even more money!

The next morning found us exploring Greenwich Village on another steamy summer day. The fact that the garbage collection was running late on the streets of lower Manhattan that day reminded me that city life was less than perfect, another useful lesson for my young grandson. Undaunted, we strolled through Union Square and checked out food and craft stalls. The crowds were large, intense, friendly, and diverse in color and dress. Rodrigo seemed energized by the swirl of activity and the whole city street scene.

As we headed down to University Place toward Washington Square Park, Rodrigo noticed a crowd gathering on a nearby sidewalk before I did. As we approached, I detected a familiar tone of voice, one with that unique New York City dialect. It reminded me of a carnival barker in the good old days in Playland in Rockaway Beach many years ago.

"Win a free bowling game," announced a man wearing a top hat and bow tie. "All you have to do is toss a beanbag through the cornhole." He then pointed to a large board set right on the sidewalk. "Step right up and give it a try."

He did not have a microphone. He did not need one. And if that was not enough of an attraction, a person of considerable size stood nearby dressed as a giant bowling pin with the inscription "Bowlmor" on his chest. Sure enough, as I looked up, I saw a sign with an arrow pointing to the bowling alley on the second floor of a nearby building.

Rodrigo watched intently as several people unsuccessfully tried their hand at tossing the beanbag into the hole. Despite his better judgment, or was it shyness, with my prodding, he did step up. Although the gathered crowd was immediately in his corner, his three tosses went awry. Turning to me, he said, "Grandpa Ken, let's see you do it." My first toss was off to the right. The second was closer. When the third toss disappeared into one of the holes on the board, there was good-natured cheering as Rodrigo and I slapped hands and high-fived each other. Even the bowling pin person walked over and joined in our little celebration as if he was one of the family. With a flourish, he presented Rodrigo with a card that said, "This game is on us, no charge. Free!"

With great expectations, Rodrigo and I went upstairs armed with our special complimentary award. Rodrigo gave the card to the staff person behind the counter. With a certain lack of enthusiasm, he said congratulations and asked for our shoe sizes. As he put the bowling shoes on the counter, he announced that they would cost sixteen dollars for each shoe rental. "We take all credit cards," he stated with a confident swagger if not haughtiness.

I was shocked. I was pissed. A small print sign on the wall listed the cost of playing a game at Bowlmor as all of ten dollars. "Thanks for nothing, buddy," I said. "This is a rip-off!" I slammed the free game certificate on the counter along with the overpriced bowling shoes. I took Rodrigo by the hand and proceeded down the steps and out of the bowling alley.

"Rodrigo," I said, "as we reached the street. "Beware of offers seemingly too good to be true. There is no such thing as a free lunch or free bowling game, especially in New York City." I explained to my grandson that charging sixteen bucks for renting bowling shoes was nothing more than a New York City scam. "A rip-off," I yelled but not before some foul words polluted the air. Seeing that I was upset, Rodrigo told me it was okay even if he did not immediately incorporate all the details. Showing resilience and with my arm around his shoulder, we proceeded down the busy street in search of a well-deserved ice cream treat. Looking up at me with affection, Rodrigo said," It's okay, Grandpa," as he hugged me.

We saw a sign for a New York City–style ice cream parlor as we walked. This upscale place was a far cry from my childhood neighborhood ice cream shops, let alone the Good Humor truck. I was appalled when I checked the prices on the wall above the counter. The minuscule size of the cones further inflamed my reaction. "This is not our kind of place," I said emphatically to my grandson. Although disappointed, he followed my lead and we departed empty-handed.

As we reached the street, I explained to Rodrigo that I had a better plan to give us more "bang for the buck." Because I had visited this neighborhood many times, I was familiar with the offerings of a nearby drugstore that carried colossal ice cream sandwiches in their freezer section. We quickly located the refreshment section and departed with our substantial one dollar treat. "Now, Rodrigo, this is value and money saved," I stated, nodding affirmatively as we walked one short block to the always busy and vibrant Washington Square Park. We found an empty bench under a delightful shade tree and watched the flow of human traffic. "There's nothing better than finding a bargain in New York City," I said as I licked chocolate from my fingers. My grandson smiled at me as he worked his way around the extra-large ice cream sandwich that was melting at an alarming rate. He laughed when I told him we would both need a shower when we got back to the apartment.

I suspect that Rodrigo will never forget our Bowlmor experience and will be wary of advertisements that appear to be too good to be true. At the same time, I am confident he gained valuable knowledge about the value of a dollar: why waste money when bargains are right around the corner?

My Hawaiian Shirt

"Please buckle your seatbelts; we will be landing in about twenty minutes," the flight attendant announced. I stretched out my legs, which now felt like three-day-old stale pretzels, and sighed with relief as some hint of circulation returned.

When I first received the invitation to speak to leaders in the Hawaiian State Legislature in 2000, I was appreciative and honored. The voice on the phone extending the invitation belonged to Kalani, a leading mental health advocate in the Aloha State. In previous years, we had attended numerous national mental health conferences together on the United States mainland and enjoyed a warm and breezy friendship. Kalani, a third-generation Hawaiian, lived life to its fullest. She was a people person who loved to flirt, laugh, and gleefully smile. She was quite the prankster, too, as I recall an episode from the previous year at a conference together in Las Vegas. I remember it vividly since I was the "victim" of a very amusing but mischievous late-night practical joke that entailed my rushing to the rescue, believing Kalani needed bail money for some bad behavior in a nearby nightclub.

On the phone call with Kalani, I was attempting to be a little coy and slightly playful myself as we first talked about the invitation to speak in Hawaii. "Kalani, I don't know; it's an awfully long trip," I whined as I attempted to mask my excitement. Kalani, a shrewd operative who did not mince words, responded by saying that I would do well to tell her now if it was too much for me. Suddenly I snapped to attention, hoping she was being playful.

"Just give me some dates, and I'll be there," I said, emphasizing "be there." It seemed like a great way to welcome and celebrate a new century!

On a cold morning in November, Kalani called me to finalize the details. "Can you come the first week of January and perhaps stay for a week or eight or nine days?" she asked. Kalani had little appreciation of the winter weather conditions in Montpelier although I had shared stories about snowstorms and blizzards. I remember, at some previous conference, regaling Kalani and other friends during a social hour gathering with stories about turning the corner on State and Main in downtown Montpelier in early January and walking towards the state capital and directly into a winter wind and frequent snowstorms. Concluding this tale, I turned to Kalani and suggested, with exaggerated contrast, that she was probably packing her car for a day at the Waikiki beach as we confronted rugged Vermont conditions.

My work assignment, she told me, would be to take several days during the first week of the year to meet with legislative leaders and prepare a presentation for both the House and Senate chambers to promote a proposed bill modeled on Vermont's 1997 parity legislation for mental health and substance abuse insurance coverage. Kalani also reminded me that she was arranging for several additional days touring the island with three days reserved for a stay on the North Shore so I could better appreciate the beauty and culture of this distant land.

With this generous offer, going to and working in Hawaii seemed as simple and no more bothersome than driving to the nearby Wayside Family Restaurant for an early-morning pancake breakfast. "Yes," I said with enthusiasm, "I can come the first week in January." We spent the next fifteen minutes discussing logistics and work details. Still, my mind and concentration were slightly diverted by images of palm trees, beaches, and maidens gently swaying in hula dresses.

It is a long haul from Montpelier to Honolulu. The plane

landed with a thud, and slowly, as the rows emptied, I made my way into the terminal. "Aloha, aloha," greeted me as I entered the arrival area and Kalani and several associates surrounded me. For sure, Kalani had a flair for the dramatic. Without warning, she and her friends threw two colorful leis over my head as they sang a traditional Hawaiian welcome song, drawing instant attention from other travelers. I was embarrassed but appreciative. I had no idea Kalani had organized a small airport welcoming party.

With a natural tendency towards drama and a sense of theater, she stepped forward and handed me a gift-wrapped package with a rather large red bow. "Open it," she said as she slid one arm around my shoulder and kissed me with dramatic flair. I carefully untied the ribbon and peeled open the box although I felt a little self-conscious in the crowded and busy airport. Inside the package was a beautiful, red, extra-large Hawaiian shirt adorned with a most attractive white flower pattern.

Although I was a casual dresser, probably "sloppy casual," with little eye for fashion, I had dutifully packed the usual white shirt, tie, and sports jacket as accouterments for my formal work. Back in Montpelier, this was expected dress for men working at the State House. Much to my pleasant surprise, Kalani told me in no uncertain terms that it would be appropriate to wear this new red shirt for my work assignments at the Hawaiian State Legislature. For a fleeting moment, I wondered whether this was one of Kalani's pranks, but others assured me that this casual dress was fitting and appropriate. My white shirt, tie, and jacket never left the bottom of my suitcase during my entire stay.

Until that day, I had never owned or worn a Hawaiian shirt. In truth, almost no one I knew in Vermont had ever appeared in such garb, and the one fellow who did was confronted with a barrage of commentary ranging from good-natured ribbing to ridicule. Over time, this shirt became my favorite, and I must admit there was a particular joy in presenting a different look.

"What's with the shirt?" asked several friends in Montpelier when I showed up for dinner at Julio's restaurant in Montpelier the following summer. While their tone was either slightly playful or somewhat caustic, the shirt set me apart from the usual Vermont suit-wearer. I relished the garment and the good memories it carried from my Hawaiian adventure.

In years to follow, the shirt became prominent in my summer wardrobe for travels near and far, and I have random photographs to prove it. I wore it on a spectacular visit to Robben Island off the coast of Cape Town in South Africa on the day I toured the site of Nelson Mandela's tiny prison cell where he lived for eighteen years before his release and election as president of the country. On a different work assignment in Africa, I am pictured with local native women selling their relatively meager crafts in a village in Swaziland as one vendor applauds my stylish Hawaiian shirt. Other photos capture me in my comfortable Hawaiian shirt on the streets of Paris, on a bike in Spain somewhere on the Costa Bravo, gazing at the Adriatic Sea in Puglia in southern Italy, and on a sun-drenched street in Copenhagen while sitting in an outdoor café with a frosty beer as a companion.

My Hawaiian shirt is front and center in an enduring photograph capturing my elderly mom on my arm as we walked on a beautiful summer morning near Packwood, Washington, with the lovely red of the shirt offset by the majestic white of snowy Mt. Rainier, which towered over us in the background.

Although one might think that the shirt carries only happy, pleasant summer memories, I wore it when my mother died in 2016 as she lay unconscious at a nearby Montpelier nursing home. The weather outside was typical for Vermont in early February: cold with occasional snow squalls followed by occasional peeks of sunshine. I sat alone with her as she slowly concluded a long life. As in most eldercare facilities, room temperatures were elevated, close to tropical conditions.

Although my mom was failing in her silent departure, I decided to open the curtains to capture the beauty of the scene outside the window. If my mother had not been dying and unaware, I am sure she would have relished the scene—of fresh snow on trees outside the window while birds fluttered in and out as they visited a nearby bird feeder. To ease the silence, pain, and sadness, while knowing how hothouse warm the rooms at the Woodridge Nursing Home were, I played a recording of Vivaldi's "The Four Seasons" on my phone but not before fumbling in my backpack, taking off a warm sweater and shirt and replacing it with . . . my special red Hawaiian shirt, which I had packed into my small bag before leaving home that morning. My mother was beyond notice, but I found comfort in this garment, which was part of my life and identity.

A year later, my partner Sarah Hofmann and I decided to get married. On an early August day, our respective children and grandchildren gathered under the old apple tree behind our house on Sparrow Farm Road. This was certainly not your typical formal wedding with limousines, tuxedos, and a fancy hotel. Still, Sarah and I managed to arrive in dashing form, riding our bicycles down our dirt road and into our back field, where our ceremony commenced under an old but still productive apple tree. Sarah, being a Midwesterner with traditional values, wore more formal attire to mark the occasion. I, on the other hand, was dressed to kill in—you guessed it—my favorite red Hawaiian shirt, complete with a celebratory bow tie!

A Bucksaw, a Scythe, and Silvia

My old barn is still standing, but like its owner, it sags a bit in places and groans under the stress of cold winds from the north, a sure sign that blankets of snow will soon arrive. On one wall, hanging from several bent and rusted nails, sits a bucksaw and, to its right, an old scythe. Both items, cherished and important nearly five decades ago, carry distant and fleeting memories like an old love affair remembered but long gone, fading into a distant past but with a warm glow nevertheless.

Recently, while looking for tires stored in my barn, I managed, much to my chagrin, to bump my head once again on the ridiculously short five-foot-high barn entranceway. As I stumbled forward rubbing my hurt, I looked up, and my eyes focused on these two old farm relics hanging silently, ignored, and neglected for decades. I was hit with a wave of nostalgia as my fingers slowly touched them, caressing the dirty and dusty outlines of the rusty bucksaw and then the scythe. There was an instant and electric connection with these tools, and they unleashed memories that linked me to my early arrival into rural Vermont life in 1976. This association with the ancient tools tied me forever with the most unlikely friend I might ever have, who—in her way—was my mentor and sometimes nemesis, marking and defining another chapter in my life.

Nearly fifty years ago, these primitive tools, both already well past their prime, were gifted to me by my eccentric, cantankerous, rugged, demanding, and reclusive neighbor who, despite our differences in background, culture, and personality, forged a friendship with me that leaped over and around boundaries.

My neighbor was a woman named Silvia Narma.

The year we met, I was a robust thirty-one-year-old fellow who, until landing here in central Vermont, had lived his entire life in urban settings, beginning with a childhood in Brooklyn and Queens in New York City. Years later, I settled in Vermont with my wife Janet and infant son Jamie, who was born in Boston. We were "flatlanders" so naïve and, in a way, innocent about our new environment that we were unfamiliar with the pejorative label and its meaning for nearly a year after our arrival. We had become Vermonters by choice, not birth, and had lots to learn.

By chance, my next-door neighbor on what was then called Gould Hill (now Sparrow Farm Road) was Silvia, who was nearly twenty years my senior. She was tough and smart but idiosyncratic, eccentric, and unique in so many ways. At first, she ignored us and our presence as if we were not her new next-door neighbors. I found this unsettling since, given our proximity, we could catch glimpses of each other on many occasions. Six months passed without any direct communication. Curious to be sure from visual sightings, Silvia toiled on her land dressed like, at least in my mind, a European peasant, adorned with a colorful, if faded, headscarf and dusty work outfits. Her daily routine consisted of planting, clearing land, hunting for mushrooms, cutting firewood, attending to her bees, and milking and caring for her beloved cow. In winter, she seemed housebound, singular, and isolated but with a steady stream of chimney smoke marking her presence.

I did notice that during these early months, Silvia seemed to lack visitors with no discernible contact with local neighbors. Although I did not mean to pry, I still found this unsettling. Silvia's old beater of a car sat out front seemingly locked in place, another layer of a mystery to be sure.

Perhaps her singular and private existence reflected much early trauma in her life. Neighbors whispered or implied when speaking about my neighbor that she was a strange woman. Several people referred to her as "the hermit lady." Certainly, Silvia was not one for small talk or casual social engagement. I discovered, in conversation with our mail person, that Silvia was originally from Estonia. It took a trip to the library to consult with a world atlas to locate this Eastern European country, which was, it seemed, near Russia and once part of Russia but now independent.

By the time I wandered up to Vermont, Silvia had long settled in an old, tired, and dilapidated house with plenty of land and trees offering quiet beauty, privacy, and solitude. Just glancing at Silvia told me she was a sturdy, powerful woman. She was short, at least a foot shorter than me, rather stout to be sure, and (pushing honesty to its limits) she might be described as built like a small Sherman tank with solid shoulders, muscular arms, and a torso that commanded attention and my respect as she attacked various physical chores and activities. She was a farmer at heart who lived close to her land and modest dwelling.

After having no communication with my neighbor for months after I moved in, it was a surprise when Silvia offered a wave and a hello as I walked past her place. At first, I was too stunned to react, but I approached and introduced myself and told her about my wife and infant son, Jamie. As I recall, we talked about the weather and the recent mud season with Silva choosing the topics. Then, much to my surprise, for some unknown reason, she invited me for coffee at her house the very next weekend morning. Why she decided to interact remains a mystery. It was a subject we never explored, but as a result, there are still endless possibilities and conjectures.

I knocked and entered her house a few days later. Her little dog King Rex, a dachshund, yelped at my feet and jumped around in a bothersome and distracting manner. A glance around Silvia's kitchen suggested she would not get a passing review from *Good Housekeeping*. There were six or seven yellow strips of sticky flypaper hanging from different sections of the kitchen ceiling, and most of them had quite a selection of dead flying insects. This diverse collection might make an entomologist swoon. But Silvia also had numerous hangings of drying herbs, plants, and flowers along with several trays of sliced apples, which added some much-needed pleasant fragrance and country ambiance.

As she talked, her face showed little emotion. Still, I could detect from her questions that she was probing, taking note of my extensive city credentials. With little-disguised disdain, she was discovering that I knew nothing about rural life or country living. At first, I felt awkward, perhaps nervous, but still, I wanted to be a good guest, so I sipped her hot coffee that was strong enough to melt my spoon. This utensil sat unused since it needed a good scrubbing, and I felt obligated to munch on some offered refreshment, a cookie of sorts that seemed to contain an amazing amount of what I discovered in later visits was lard. She augmented these refreshments with a few chopped dried apples, a welcome respite.

From the start, we were strange bedfellows. To say that she was eccentric would be an understatement. Her unusual persona and lifestyle were exemplified by the fact that her beloved cow, formally named Cow, was allowed to hang out on and, to be more exact, *in* her side porch room, an enclosed porch next to her kitchen separated only by a half door.

As I sat and visited during those first weeks of our fragile but budding friendship, Silvia hosted me in her kitchen with steaming hot coffee and some unfamiliar and frequently barely edible treats. Our initial conversations focused on local weather reports and the antics of her beloved Cow. Soon, she expanded her conversation to lecture me about the proper way to gather and cut firewood or about planting and caring for a vegetable garden. The following week, she took me outside and taught me the best method for collecting manure out on her hillside. My visits became more frequent, and as they did, Silvia proved to be most capable of testing my knowledge and abilities. To her credit, she showed no reserve in some harsh and critical commentary about my shortcomings. In her own way, her personality matched her coffee—strong, slightly bitter, and, at times, overpowering. Despite some awkward and uncomfortable moments, I was intrigued and marched up to her place with anticipation, entering an unfamiliar environment that seemed distant from my urban upbringing. In her singular way, she was becoming my mentor and teacher.

After several months, I became more acclimated to Silvia's house and lifestyle. She always insisted that I have a cup of coffee, and although I worried her strong coffee might burn a hole in my stomach, I drained it down. One saving grace was the realization that I could temper the naturally bitter coffee taste by adding fresh and local milk supplied that very morning by Cow. Frankly, Silvia's house smelled like, well, a barn, and I was eternally grateful that she kept fresh hay on the porch floor which served to mute, if not eliminate, the rather distinct aroma of fresh cow manure.

On a spring day that year, Silvia informed me over her kitchen table that buying wood for my stove was unnecessary. "Foolish," she said with her face slightly contorted for emphasis. This instruction came after I told her about my first recent wood delivery by a local elderly fellow. It was old Mr. Kane who delivered stovewood, charging me forty dollars for a cord. This seemed like an excessive amount, but what did I know? I provided Silvia with further detail, telling how Mr. Kane recalled that as a boy, he visited my house with his mother as the owner, Annie Gould, lay dying. With a certain delight, Mr. Kane showed me where the spittoon was located in the Gould living room. Silvia laughed when I confessed that I had no idea about what a spittoon was and that I had to look it up at the Kellogg-Hubbard Library in Montpelier.

Silvia informed me that it was time to prepare firewood for

the coming season. She provided me with a lecture about the difference between green and dry wood. Under her tutelage, I started as her assistant up in her woods as she found and cut small logs and big branches and proceeded to slice stove-size pieces with a bucksaw. I am not sure I had ever seen a bucksaw and certainly not one in action. This hand tool was uncomplicated, and I was eager to be educated. I must admit Silvia made it look easy as her strong arms sawed and cut, as her body swayed slightly. My job was to haul long and sometimes heavy branches—which she had prepared weeks, perhaps months, in advance—down from her land. Within an hour, her pile of firewood was impressive. Then, as I complimented her, she invited me to try some cutting. It took me a while to get a feel for sawing with the bucksaw. What I lacked in experience, I made up with enthusiasm although my mentor showed impatience at my slow learning curve. I had age and vigor on my side, and besides, my frugal nature made this cost-effective exercise most appealing, a good workout for an athletic guy.

Several days later, Silvia waved to me from her front yard, signaling that she was inviting me to come up and visit. She took me to a shed she had out back which was filled with an assortment of old tools and a jumble of odds and ends. She moved some tools around and pulled out an old bucksaw under a pile of junk, and to my surprise, she presented it to me as a gift. I accepted it with appreciation. I sensed that Silvia was not inclined to offer presents. I was moved by her gratitude and gift.

I tramped through my ten acres of land all spring and summer, cutting and dragging logs and long branches down to my barn, where I set up my bucksaw operation. This was a primitive activity, and although my saw was below standard, the process did have virtue. I noticed, with manly pride, that my arm muscles seemed to relish exercise, and although it was a slow process, there was a pleasure in seeing my little woodpile grow and expand as the warm summer days began to retreat to the cooling September mornings. Silvia came by, examined my work, and nodded as I hauled the wood down to my house in my wheelbarrow. No words of approval were spoken, but I took pleasure in her affirmative shake of her head as she reviewed my work.

Silvia first explained to me that wood was a great source of heat. I detected a slight smile, something that did not come easy to her. She explained that you first were warmed by sawing and cutting wood, then when you split and stacked it, and again when hauling it to the house. She confessed that one of her great pleasures was sitting by the stove in her living room and feeling its warmth on a cold winter's night. Now that sounded good to me.

That year I made several new friends in town, and they were amazed when I shared my tale of buck-sawing firewood. I suspect that this "primitive approach" provided some comic relief to a couple of my new buddies. Still, one earnest fellow who lived in central Vermont all his life felt obligated to bring over his gas-powered chain saw and give me a demonstration. I was certainly impressed with its speed and efficiency. I purchased a chain saw the following spring. Knowing that Silvia would disapprove, I waited until the following year to use it. Sure enough, within an hour, Silvia found me up in the woods with my new noisy saw. She said nothing, but disapproval was written all over her face.

My relationship with Silvia took form and shape during my second summer in Vermont. While she was a private person, little by little, details of her life slipped out and appeared like lilac blossoms in early spring. She shared with me details of her early life in Estonia and the discord of World War II when she fled to America. To my surprise, she informed me that she was operating an informal business—more of a distribution service—out of her house as she circulated Estonian newspapers, magazines, and books stored in her dirt-filled basement to patriots throughout America. However, all the material was received and eventually distributed to and from the post office in Waterbury rather than Montpelier. Silvia indicated that she wanted to elude detection, so rather than rely on the Montpelier Post Office, she picked up material ten miles north and mailed publications from there regularly.

One day, she inquired whether I traveled to Waterbury much. "Often," I said since most state offices, including the Department of Mental Health, were there. I could tell she had an ulterior motive. This would become more apparent in the following year when the backseat of my car was frequently loaded with outgoing material from Silvia to Estonian refugees across America or messy piles of publications smuggled out of Estonia and intended for Silvia and her homemade distribution center. The Waterbury Post Office staff considered me a regular customer over the course of many years.

While Silvia was a woman of strong opinions, capable of giving blunt assessments on subjects large and small, she had other interesting, if unexplained, ways of making mischief. One day she greeted and shocked me by wearing the most realistic bear costume I had ever seen. I was impressed, but she refused to explain why and how she had secured such an item. Once, and only once, did Silvia wear this outfit in public, creating quite a stir and fright in our neighborhood. And I would be her accomplice as we surprised a nearby neighbor who was hosting a large summer party in their yard.

One summer day in 1980, my secretary at work relayed an emergency message from Silvia that said she needed my help immediately. I drove home and found her sitting at her kitchen table with papers scattered. With pen in hand, she explained the emergency to me. She told me that during the noontime news on local radio station WDEV, they had mentioned that a sailing competition in the Summer Olympics was being held in Russia. Silvia was certain that the sailing event was taking place in Estonia, and she wanted WDEV to clarify that Estonia was no longer part of Russia. "You must drive up to WDEV and give them this letter I have written," commanded Silvia. And so I did. Together, Silvia and I listened to the late afternoon news on WDEV and rejoiced when they read her letter on the air.

Silvia was not a subtle person, so I did not take umbrage when she informed me that I was to help her hay a nearby field on the coming Saturday. By then, I had gotten accustomed to her dictates and direct, unfiltered, even brusque commands. At the same time, she signaled appreciation towards me when she delivered a large container of fresh honey, which I greatly enjoyed.

On the assigned day for our haying project, I woke up early, feeling slightly resistant to the unknown assignment but also intrigued by this task. From what Silvia implied, this effort would primarily be for the benefit of Cow, so how could I say no?

It was already warm, bordering on hot, when we met well before nine the following morning. According to Silvia, the conditions were perfect with ample sunshine, a cloudless sky, and dry summer weather in the forecast. Her work outfit reflected her casual approach to dress. She wore old, clunky, beaten work boots and slightly ripped, dirty long pants highlighted by a University of Connecticut basketball practice T-shirt that hung down long enough to also serve as a nightgown if Silvia was so inclined. I had given her this present after she dug up one of her beloved yellow Globeflower plants for me to add to my expanding flower garden. I knew she managed on a modest income and spent not a penny on clothes, cleaning materials, or perfumes, at least as far as I could detect. Since I was not one to throw things away, I had quite a collection of tattered, old practice jerseys from college basketball days, so one less would be of no consequence, and seeing her in my old basketball top was a joyful bonding moment for me.

Silvia carried a primitive-looking scythe along with a large rake down from her house to the nearby open field. Seeing Silvia standing out in this lush, green expanse with her scythe hanging loosely over her shoulder made a pleasant picture, but I knew nothing about this primitive field tool. The closest I had come to learning about or appreciating a scythe was when I visited the Boston Museum of Fine Arts years ago and admired some paintings of pastoral, rural scenes in the European gallery.

Handing me the rake, Silvia told me to follow her closely as she proceeded to make a straight first row of cut grass in the large field. Despite Silvia's rather bulky frame, her movements were graceful as she turned and sliced the high grass, seemingly without great effort but with a steady rhythm as she glided across the field. My job, a task almost beyond my capacity, was to keep up with her progress, raking the sweetly smelling, freshly cut grass into mounds and piles for later collection.

The morning heat penetrated, and we worked silently but in sync. By noon, I was sweating profusely, lathered up like a galloping horse as Silvia charged ahead, her bandanna and jersey stained with perspiration. Finally, she called for a break and opened a jug of water for us to share. Taking off my shirt, I squeezed the soaked covering and laughed. We must have looked like quite a pair, a decidedly odd couple out in the field. I noticed one or two cars slow down and stop, taking in the scene as we worked, but they proceeded down the hill without comment. I now wish I had a snapshot of Silvia moving with resolve with her scythe with me raking alongside, shirtless with my back turning brown, looking like a giant next to the much shorter Silvia, a human Sherman tank, swinging with grace, power, and purpose.

I returned to my house to get a couple of baloney sandwiches and washed them down with a cold soda. Silvia went up to her place and later reported that she had curdled cheese, dried apples, honey with nuts, and home-brewed peppermint tea.

Completing this short break, we met at the nearby field, and Silvia offered me a chance to try out the scythe. I was up to the challenge, although my hands were rubbed raw from the vigorous raking all morning. What had seemed so natural and effortless for Silvia was more than unfamiliar and uncomfortable for me. Swinging the blade horizontally and making an accurate cut was much more challenging. I was prone to either slicing nothing but air or, even worse, swinging too low and kicking up dirt. With hands on her ample hips, Silvia offered suggestions, barking them out in a way that reminded me of my high school basketball coach. Her words were both critical and encouraging, so I tried to follow her instructions. Soon, I had a smoother, more efficient, and more effective cutting style, and although my rows were not as straight as hers, they were acceptable.

Later in the afternoon, Silvia went to her house and returned with several large, old, tattered blankets. Together we set them out and piled mounds of drying hay and grass into the center area. Silvia carefully tied the ends, and we took turns throwing them over our shoulders and carrying these bundles up to her side porch and shed where the hay would be stored for future feedings.

At this moment, I experienced an unsettling feeling, for as I tossed one hay bale with extra force, I sensed some stirring in the far end of the shed. Wiping sweat out of my eyes, I thought I glimpsed some movement, something large like a rodent. At first, I assumed it was a family of mice, but they seemed too robust. I was startled to realize that they might be a pack of rats. Since I was uncertain, I said nothing to Silvia but my body felt on high alert.

Doubting myself and calming my worries, I slowly walked home. Every bone in my body felt depleted, but there was a sense of having put in a full day's work. As I trudged up from the field with my last bundled load, the image of the pastoral scene in the Boston Museum reoccurred, but this time, I pictured myself in the frame.

A day or two later, when I went out early in the morning to get the daily paper, I was surprised to find an old, dilapidated, slightly broken scythe sitting by the side porch door. Once again, Silvia must have sorted through the jumble of old tools and remnants of her farm instruments to dig out this item. There was no note or words exchanged when I saw her next, but I took it as an act of friendship and appreciation for my effort.

Together, Silvia and I repeated this task once more that summer. It was exhausting work, but I enjoyed the physical labor and the sense of completion, not to mention the heavy exertion. Best of all, we had a sense of bonding as we toiled under the warming Vermont summer sun.

A neighbor down the road who had a small farm operation must have taken note or perhaps pity. For the next several years, this farmer and his boys used their tractor to cut the hay in our nearby field and then bundled it. My job was limited to helping them throw the hay bales into a pickup truck and then pile them in Silvia's shed. Silvia seemed slightly conflicted and somewhat grumpy about this turn of events, but I, for one, did not complain.

Although Silvia was reticent to share information about herself or her past, there was a hot summer night, probably four years into our friendship, where we sat on my front lawn and had a revealing conversation. Although she did not drink or smoke—that night, she did both. As she downed not one but several beers, the lush evening air combined with the alcohol seemed to open the floodgates and memories poured out. She shared with me the details of her turbulent earlier days in Estonia. With laser-like recall, she talked about fighting against the Russian occupation of her homeland. She went on, sipping the beer as if it were iced tea, to relate details of her exploits including direct physical combat and acts of terrorism against the occupation force. Silvia, with eyes becoming watery, told me of her pain in fleeing her homeland and becoming a displaced young woman who eventually found her way to America. When she implied, more with hints than specifics, that she had used her hands to disable, or was it strangle, a Russian soldier who had uncovered her underground activities, I silently ingested this shocking revelation, a subject we never referred to or mentioned again. It was too personal and painful for both of us.

Now, decades later, the bucksaw and scythe hang silently in the barn with little utility or worth. Seven years ago, my wife Sarah and I had an extensive cleanup campaign at the house and in the barn. At first, I inspected each item carefully, but after a week of labor, we tossed old things away with reckless abandon. I almost removed the two old farm implements and added them to the large dumpster. It was then that I realized that old keepsakes have great value in treasured memories, if not monetary worth, allowing me to reminisce and write about the past. The bucksaw and scythe remain in view, too precious and meaningful to discard, recalling days passed with my exceptional neighbor.

The Big Picture on Big Pharma

I entered Central Vermont Medical Center as the COVID-19 epidemic swept through Vermont and the country. It was with mixed emotions that I proceeded to the designated area for vaccinations. The promise of a COVID-19 vaccine was uplifting. It felt like I was being given a key to a door marked, "Enter with care: new normal straight ahead." Or so I thought.

Being in the seventy-five-and-older club made me eligible for a gold-club-like status as I joined other elderly folks in the first group to receive the vaccine. I could not help but notice that my compatriots were not the same vigorous folks I remember from the Woodstock days. In fact, the super senior club maintained a rather silent vigil as individuals shuffled along to designated cubicles.

After months, weeks, and days of dread, feeling vulnerable, and nearly a year of being socially isolated from family and living like a captive sentenced to an uncertain future, the shot offered hope. As the nurse injected the vaccine, I felt a deep wave of relief and immediately inquired about the second dose. The nurse gave me the information and added these fateful words, "You can thank Pfizer."

I felt gratitude that several pharmaceutical companies had created an antidote for the dreaded COVID-19 virus. Because of my long history of interaction with this industry, I have confidence that companies such as Pfizer, AstraZeneca, and Johnson & Johnson will take full credit for saving me and the rest of the world. But there is more to the story.

For decades, I have been a public critic of the pharmaceutical industry. They are, in my opinion, the robber barons of the twenty-first century with policies and practices that have enriched their coffers at the expense of consumers who need and rely on their products. Their vast resources buy them overwhelming political and economic power, which means no one except the industry can set prices for their products, a reality that negatively impacts the lives of every American now and into the future. Big Pharma has enormous influence and sway in Congress, state legislative bodies, and the medical-industrial complex. Doctors and medical institutions have also been victimized by the industry's iron grip, but all too often, they have become co-conspirators in a corrupt system.

Despite cries for reform and regulation, Congress has done little. One feeble response has been a requirement that the industry list possible side effects of the many new drugs that have flooded the marketplace. In recent decades, the drug companies have assumed a strategy of marketing medications through advertising. One cannot watch an evening TV show without hearing about new pharmaceutical products with a litany of possible side effects that include fainting spells, dizziness, irregular heartbeat, and erections lasting days, not to mention bouts of vomiting or diarrhea.

Over the years, I became aware of the industry's success marketing medications that focus on behavioral health conditions. Using various marketing techniques, including gifts and payments to every sector of the medical community, the industry made psychotropic medications the first line of treatment throughout the country, and this resulted in an excessive level of prescriptions. The pharmaceutical industry encouraged the further expansion of the marketplace by promoting "off-labeling" of products, which encouraged the prescribing of medications beyond their approved uses by the Food and Drug Administration. Excessive levels of overreliance followed as did profiteering.

As a result, in Vermont, reliance on psychotropic medications skyrocketed, impacting patients of all ages. Vulnerable populations, ranging from children and adolescents in the state's Medicaid program to Vermont elders in nursing homes, suffered from overprescribing. This approach even infiltrated Vermont's correctional system, where inmates have been inundated with questionable prescription practices.

In one of the very few public censures, at least until the more recent Purdue Pharma scandal in 2009, the United States Department of Justice announced that Pfizer had been fined $2.3 billion for the illegal promotion of many of their pharmaceutical products. The findings included the improper use of off-labeling products and kickbacks paid to healthcare providers.

The year 2009 was a big year for beginning to address the issue in Vermont. I was one of the instigators in a proposed major bill intended to institute the strictest rules in the nation regarding marketing activities by the pharmaceutical and medical device industries. The legislation called for a ban on all gifts from the industry to the state's medical community along with a required public disclosure of any expenditures.

There was a pitched battle all winter in the State House with pharma devoting time, resources, and lobbyists to defeat the measure. However, our citizen legislature was particularly moved to support the bill when it was revealed that, in 2008, Vermont doctors received $3 million in gifts from pharmaceutical companies although there was no public identification of the recipients. The information was shielded from public view.

The bill passed and was signed into law by Governor Jim Douglas in June of 2009. In addition to the statewide media coverage, *The New York Times* called Vermont's bill "the most stringent state effort to regulate marketing and to change the relationship between pharmaceutical companies and doctors."

Now, ten years from Vermont's successful campaign to contain the pharmaceutical industry, I dutifully returned to the Central Vermont Medical Center for my second Pfizer shot, feeling that

I was being released from bondage. Little did I suspect at the time that I would have to return for a booster shot amid growing uncertainty about the nature and scope of the pandemic.

Thanking Pfizer and other companies for finding a remedy to the COVID-19 virus is appropriate, but so too is the realization that until we get control over the pharmaceutical industry, access to affordable healthcare is impossible.

A Challenging Special Birthday

The morning sun was hiding behind some early fog, but the sky was already showing patches of deep blue while a gentle ocean breeze occasionally made the house curtains stir. It was a near-perfect start to a special day in Aquinnah, a town formerly known as Gay Head, that sits on the very western tip of Martha's Vineyard.

My new partner and love, Sarah Hofmann, was celebrating her birthday on the second day of July 2009. It was Sarah's first visit to this lush, romantic island, and I wanted the occasion to be a unique, unforgettable celebration. Our relationship was only months old, so we both could see and feel nothing but perfection in each other. We were not fooled by the moment but willing to revel in the life-affirming experience of new love. I was past sixty by several years, and Sarah was nearly a dozen years my junior. Defying age and perhaps reason, we were, at that moment, kids at heart.

My imaginary Rolodex of island restaurants appropriate for a birthday dinner was slim. My frugal nature automatically eliminated some high-end places, including several that did not even bother listing their prices. Over many years, my penchant for eating and cooking in had provided limited exposure to the island's endless culinary choices. One exception was the restaurant up on the cliffs of Gay Head, just a mile up the road. This setting was a delight for breakfast, especially outside on the deck overlooking the ocean, but the dinner menu was limited and somewhat uninspired.

Knowing that Sarah was more inclined to enjoy a good meal in a well-appointed eatery, I threw caution to the wind and reserved a table at the Homeport Restaurant in the nearby fishing village of Menemsha. This place was a favorite of my now departed mother, who loved seafood, especially lobsters. Every time she ate there with her dear friend Jean, it was a celebration. Not only was the seafood fresh and delicious, but the setting was superb.

The Homeport had many virtues. It served seafood fresh off the fishing boats docked by the pier. Based on reputation, they provided ample portions and managed to keep the prices reasonable. Located on Menemsha Pond, the restaurant was rustic with a pleasing Cape Cod charm. In the evening, the sun set directly to the west, providing vibrant sunset colors on the surrounding water, which also blanketed everyone inside with a special summer glow.

When I told Sarah of my choice for dinner, she was thrilled. As I explained, Aquinnah and Menemsha were almost connected, but a strong current, absent a bridge or connecting road, separated the two towns at the closest point, making the two-minute swim improbable if not unsafe. So, like most visitors, we would have to drive the six miles to Menemsha, which meant traversing hilly and winding roads, a short trip with many spectacular views of the ocean and ponds along the way. This meant passing through the village of Chilmark, turning at Beetlebung Corner, and then dipping into Menemsha, a tiny, charming town with fishermen, artists, and tourists ever present. Sarah soaked up the information like she did the sun.

We decided to start our day with a bike ride to the nearby beach on this birthday morning. Cycling to Philbin Beach meant an initial uphill climb that culminated near the Gay Head Lighthouse, but the reward was a spectacular downhill glide with the ocean in full display. Parking our bikes, we quickly settled on our beach towels and took in the view. Just a short distance away were the colorful Gay Head Cliffs and the stunning lighthouse with its constant beacon. The ocean waves rolled constantly, sometimes wild and rough and sometimes gentle. Before noon, the beach was nearly empty. The ocean was inviting, and we waded in. Sarah was clearly the strongest swimmer, but I pushed myself to keep up as we managed to move beyond the crashing surf. Soon we were floating on our backs up and over the ocean waves as the sun beat down. We were, at that moment, a sun-kissed couple.

When we returned to the cottage for a late lunch, I secretly slid a bottle of white wine into the refrigerator, hiding it from Sarah's view. I knew little about selecting wine, but a bottle listed at nine dollars with an attractive label seemed a good choice. I rationalized this selection by assuming that Sarah could appreciate a man who knew the value of a dollar. We exchanged wet bathing suits for simple summer garb and spent the next hour snacking, reading, and chatting. We then headed outside for our car trip. A midafternoon departure would give ample time for sightseeing and perhaps a walk out on the Menemsha jetty. I was a man with a plan and with a desire to impress this woman who was attractive, funny, full of energy, and ready for adventures.

We buckled our car seatbelts in the parking area at our little Aquinnah cottage. As I turned the key, but there was no response, just silence. I tried again and then a third time. Silence. Although I am not a mechanic or car expert, I did—in this case—recognize the dreaded silence of a dead battery. The nearest gas station was miles away. We were suddenly in free fall.

I am not sure I went into panic mode, but indeed, I was upset and unhappy. Sarah, with her pleasant midwestern demeanor and upbeat personality, was much calmer. After giving the steering wheel one last bang with my open hand, I cursed profanely and muttered something about canceling our Homeport dinner reservation. Sarah assured me that we would figure something out, which provided relief even if I was dubious. The first thing that came into my mind was to cycle up to the cliffs for a mundane hamburger dinner at the Aquinnah Shop Restaurant.

Sarah's response was muted. I could tell she was disappointed at the prospect of burgers and fries when I had hinted, promised, a special lobster feast at the Homeport.

I suddenly remembered that a new bike ferry had recently begun service from the tip of Aquinnah on Lobsterville Road directly across the water to the nearby Menemsha dock. This ferry was all of a two-minute voyage, and it could have been a solution to our now-canceled car ride. Abandoning the dead auto, we set out on our bikes and raced to the bike ferry, a three-mile jaunt. Despite the hectic departure, I remembered to bring our bottle of wine. Sarah, a strong and vigorous cyclist, got there first, and I could tell from her facial expression as I rode up next to her that there was a problem. She pointed to the sign with a distinct frown on her face; it indicated that the last bike ferry across was scheduled for four o'clock. It was now nearly half past four.

Things looked bleak. I was out of ideas and disappointed. I did notice, however, a small motorboat anchored nearby, tied to the small dock that the bike ferry also utilized. Although it seemed like a wasted effort, I yelled out a *hello*! To my surprise, an older man appeared from the indoor cockpit. He waved hello but showed little interest. Perhaps he had no choice at that moment but to listen to me prattle on about our troubles. I rehashed the issue of having a dead car battery, our rushed but failed attempt to catch the bike ferry, and, most of all, my despair over the ruined celebration plan for Sarah's birthday dinner at the Homeport Restaurant in Menemsha. He took it in without comment. Then I asked, more like a beggar in posture, if he might bring us across to Menemsha on his boat along with our bikes. He looked at me, then at Sarah, and, after a silent pause, said he would but with a toll charge equal to the bike ferry. Never have I been so happy to pay an overpriced fee!

The trip took a minute or two but was not without drama. While the new bike ferry had a loading dock on both sides of the channel, a regular small motorboat could not so easily or quickly unload two bicycles and passengers. We were positioned well below the Menemsha dock, but Sarah, exhibiting strength and agility, hoisted herself up. Then, with some strain, I lifted our bikes up to her. While her light bike was no problem, my heavy bicycle caused significant challenges. As I lifted it above my head, there was a critical moment when it seemed that it might fall directly into the rushing water. It would have been both an embarrassment and a disaster if the current had carried it out to Vineyard Sound. Fate was on our side. Sarah was able, with effort, to reach down low and lift the bike to safety, along with our celebratory bottle of wine, which bounced around in my bike basket none the worse for wear. With a burst of adrenaline, I hauled myself onto the pier aided by Sarah's strong arm, which held me steady and remained over my shoulder in a casual but welcome embrace.

We needed a few minutes to collect ourselves as we celebrated our unusual arrival in Menemsha. There was time to walk out on the jetty and then stroll along the public beach. Best of all, we sat near several fishing boats and watched as they unloaded their catch at the two popular fish markets in town. The Vineyard Sound was calm as we began to relax. Talking about our adventurous trip with so many twists and turns, we laughed like a couple of kids.

As the sun began to lower, we made our way to the nearby Homeport Restaurant, confirmed our reservation, and were promptly seated. It was with gratitude that I nodded my head affirmatively when the waitress asked if she could open the nine-dollar bottle of white wine that survived our demanding trip.

I was quite taken with Sarah and the way she handled this adventure. Dealing with stress and problems reveals much about a person, and she exhibited grace, not to mention a level head, under pressure. We both took pleasure in ordering a full lobster dinner. Our succulent meal, augmented with hors d'oeuvres that Sarah selected, met all birthday expectations, and our wine gave us comfort. After settling the bill, we walked out arm in arm into the dusk. It was still warm outside but not unpleasant. We both glowed from the Martha's Vineyard sun augmented by the romance now flowing from our mutual attraction. Standing on the Menemsha pier as the sun set, I gathered Sarah in my arms and kissed her in a warm embrace. With a smile on my face, I told her I had arranged for the full moon that was now rising in the darkening sky.

The one thing we had not contemplated was how we would return to our cottage in Aquinnah. We went back to the Homeport Restaurant and asked for advice. They suggested we probably needed a cab but mentioned that our bikes might pose a problem. I had some vague idea of how much a cab would charge and knew that it would dwarf the cost of our dinner. Knowing that the Vineyard has an extensive public bus system linking one town with another, we found a schedule outside in a small kiosk. Given the evening hour, we ruled it out as an option since the connections were uneven at night and it looked unlikely that we could secure the last bus to Aquinnah.

Sarah offered a different solution. Without hesitation, she suggested that we ride our bikes home. Perhaps the sultry air, the wine, the lingering taste of lobster, or her adventurous nature contributed to this challenging proposal. I was seduced by her willingness and ability to offer a rather unexpected idea, but it seemed like a creative, if slightly reckless, solution to our dilemma.

And so, like two teenagers on a particularly romantic date, we unlocked our bikes and started pedaling home but not before Sarah pulled out two small bike lights from her bag. They provided little illumination but served to alert night drivers on this back road that bikers were out late. The trip from Menemsha to Aquinnah is a challenging ride during the day with some steep, rolling hills and roads that constantly twist and turn. Doing it at night was exciting, difficult, and not without danger.

As we rode, pedaling vigorously up steep hills, our faces glistened in the warm evening air. The roads between the towns have no streetlights and few houses, so we made our way by the illumination of the full moon, which occasionally disappeared behind billowing clouds. When that occurred, it seemed like someone had turned off the lights. We were both attentive to the surroundings, and at several points along the way, we could see the moonlight reflecting off the nearby Atlantic Ocean in a spectacular display. This was a magnificent sight and a magical evening.

We made steady progress as we pedaled to State Road, the only road to the western tip of the island, and as we weaved and climbed and dipped down hills on our way toward Aquinnah. We both cheered when we passed the Aquinnah Road sign on this dark, lonely trip. Several miles from our cottage, we reached Lobsterville Road and began a very steep descent as a billowing cloud momentarily darkened our way. Our bikes picked up speed as we rushed downhill, heading closer to the water. The air became noticeably cooler, and the slightly moist ocean refreshed us. Finally, as we pedaled into our cottage driveway, we dismounted our bikes. We were, in a word, giddy.

I am not sure Sarah and I will ever have such a romantic, crazy, and reckless birthday celebration again. But the shared memory of this adventure will be with us always.

Circus Dreams

Is there a young person who has not been tempted by the allure, attraction, and theater of the circus? Images of jugglers, high trapeze acts, acrobats, animal performances, and circus clowns, not to mention the varied carnival barkers with their games of chance, float through the mind like an old-fashioned slide show on a projector.

Is there a teenager or young adult among us who has not fantasized about running away to join a circus troupe populated with other young performers who travel far and wide, pushing themselves to the limit—while performing for rapt audiences offering wild applause?

What adolescent, when viewing a circus performance, has failed to feel the beautiful tension of performers on high wires or those exotic and fierce animals or jugglers tossing balls, pins, and even knives with confidence and reckless abandon? Circus performers are mostly young and attractive, displaying rippling physical attributes as they prance and leap, twist, soar, tumble, and spin with fantastic speed and balance. The men wear outfits that become them—with tight shirts and pants accentuating their muscled and toned bodies. The women are adorned with colorful and revealing dresses or leotards, highlighting their youthful, near-perfect bodies as they entertain and perform.

I was probably ten or eleven when I saw the Ringling Brothers Circus in the old Madison Square Garden in New York City. It was stimulating and exciting, with not one but three rings, often accompanied by music, dazzling colors, and continuous action.

I remember three things from that evening. The first was that

I was allowed to have a large container of popcorn, so large that as I climbed into my seat, I spilled nearly half of the contents onto the floor. The hoots and laughter of nearby seatmates were humiliating, but I recovered in time to . . . fall in love, puppy love to be sure, with a beautiful trapeze artist with a foreign name like Mareka who soared above on the high wire to my shrieks and those of the crowd. As she ended her performance, she blew kisses, and I was so enraptured that I thought her last kiss was aimed at me! Somehow, I managed to wave back vigorously without spilling any more popcorn.

My favorite act, however, was the jugglers who tossed and exchanged an assortment of items with incredible timing and precision. There was tension in the air with each toss. Even though I had little religious orientation, I almost prayed that they would be error-free as each unfolding act offered more complications and challenges.

Decades later, I have managed to still fantasize about my imagined role in a circus. I even constructed a series of short videos in my mind. These videos show me as a virile and nimble gymnast, a strongman hoisting and then catching comely trapeze artists as they fly and prance above, and as a juggler of knives, clubs, and, yes, three basketballs—all tossed with grace and precision. I even pictured myself as the loud and commanding ringmaster. And in these daydreams, I soak up the adoration and applause, relishing the ambiance as one does a loaf of French bread and the delicious remnants of a large bowl of seafood stew.

While still in this hallucinating state, I told myself that someday I would enter the circus world with crowds of people cheering me on. And I wonder, If I can hold on to this daydream, can others keep their fantasies alive too?

Life often reveals itself in unexpected ways. Now, looking back at life through a rearview mirror, I find that events unfolded in a way that allowed me to turn a long-held daydream into a real-life experience.

In the early 1980s, I was in love with a beautiful, talented, willowy, and tall German woman with long dark hair that made me think of the fairy tale of Rapunzel. She lived her younger years in the city of Darmstadt, in what was then West Germany, and went to college in Berlin before making her way to Vermont. Although English was her second language, she was a quick learner and astute in many facets of life. Her natural artistic flair was expressed in unique and noticeable ways: painting, composition, and clothing design. Therefore, it was not surprising that she sold creative handmade scarves in local stores for a brief period. She knew no limits. She even dabbled in circus-type outfits that were small enough for a child and large enough for a man my size: tall, extra-large.

Several years earlier, my first wife, Janet, and I had divorced, and we were working hard to construct a positive environment for our young son Jamie. I was just getting established in my career. I had secured a position as director of the Vermont Association for Mental Health and found the work challenging and worthwhile. Within a couple of years, I was a fixture at the State House, lobbying and advocating for improved and expanded services for those coping with mental health conditions and on an extensive range of topics including services for children in Vermont. It did seem that I had a natural flair for presenting essential and sometimes controversial policy issues while finding compelling ways to influence decisions on funding and programming.

When Gabrielle and I first met, we were powerfully attracted to each other. But I was not the most reliable and faithful partner. In response, Gabrielle broke off our relatively new relationship and moved to Washington, DC, where she lived and worked for a year. We did see each other on occasion and eventually reconciled. It was a happy day when Gabrielle moved back to Vermont and we settled in my old farmhouse.

Always keen on challenges and adventures, Gabrielle secured

a new position with the popular local Two Penny Theater upon her return. It was a small but talented organization. It began in Plainfield in the early 1970s at Goddard College under the direction of respected local actor Donny Osman. In 1981, the theater moved its headquarters to downtown Montpelier. Two Penny did all original shows including commedia dell'arte, an early form of Italian comedy. Traveling throughout New England and the eastern United States, they also specialized in mime, comedy, clowning, and juggling with an array of funny and crazy stories that delighted audiences of all ages.

Since Gabrielle and I were both working in town, it was not unusual for me to stop by to visit my heartthrob at the Two Penny Theater headquarters on Langdon Street. I frequently visited her in her small office. I could not help but hear and notice the Two Penny actors as they prepared for work in the main room. Not only was mime central to their craft but their juggling and clowning acts were also innovative and engaging aspects of their repertoire. At times, the rehearsals were intense with egos and juggling clubs both up in the air. I was in awe of these young performers and a bit intimidated, but slowly, I got to know them. On one fateful day, I dropped my hesitancy and reservation, and in a quiet moment, I asked one actor to show me the basics of juggling. He was receptive, and I quickly discovered an enormous difference between *watching* someone with a complex skill and *trying to learn* that skill.

From that day on, I was drawn—like a moth to a naked lightbulb—to this theatrical environment and to learning and conquering the basics of juggling. I did not ask for further help, but I observed the actors at work, and perhaps through a process of osmosis, I secretly and in private began to develop some basic routines with an emphasis on balancing three balls in the air. Nothing came easy, but within several months, I could juggle confidently and even add some more advanced moves as I created dialogue and storytelling for my emerging routine.

My young son, Jamie, took great pleasure in watching me practice. And to keep him from getting bored, I added some juvenile, comic patter and storylines with happy outcomes. His laughter warmed my heart even when I dropped things or forgot my lines. Gabrielle also supported my efforts and threatened to make me a special outfit if I kept progressing.

Many people are familiar with the Ringling Bros. and Barnum & Bailey Circus. For me, the local annual Bob Jackman Variety Talent Show here in Central Vermont captured my attention, representing the pinnacle of my modest circus career. Bob was a longtime veteran of the Montpelier School system and was a great proponent of acting, music, and theater. He put together an annual extravaganza to celebrate vaudeville and circus arts, playing not at Madison Square Garden but in the packed auditoriums at Montpelier High School and Spaulding High School in Barre. Each school had two separate weekend performances, and since most of the performers came from within a fifty-mile radius, family and friends packed the venues with enthusiastic vigor. Performers ranged widely in age and skill levels, but all seemed excited to be participants.

Bob heard about my fledgling talents and invited me to be part of his next variety show, explaining that he had four other jugglers prepared to perform. Imagine my excitement when I shared the news with Gabrielle and Jamie. It was Gabrielle who suggested that I incorporate Jamie into my juggling act. Although shy and reserved, Jamie acquiesced. Our little act consisted of my juggling different items while Jamie, looking like a circus pro in his engaging clown outfit, crawled through and around my legs, using animated arm motions to encourage crowd reaction. The choreography and costumes were well received with ringing applause in response.

Our performance probably lasted no more than seven minutes each night. Still, with the glare of stage lights, the sea of people in the darkened and filled auditorium, and the crowd's roar as we finished, I felt the warmth and pleasure of pursuing and capturing a long-held dream.

Our juggling act was midway through an extensive nightly schedule of events that included tumbling, magic tricks, several clown acts, and even a low-wire balancing walk performed by a trio of young girls. But it was the act that preceded ours that riveted my attention. In this performance, a young man mastering the art of illusion appeared to saw his wife in half to the amazement of the audience. It was spectacular entertainment, and I was in awe but not ready to add this to my routine. Gabrielle, as I recall, showed little enthusiasm. Besides having Jamie as my sidekick, I remember that I did not drop one of my juggling balls during our four performances, and somehow, the young woman in the act proceeding ours survived being sawed in half without so much as a scratch!

That year, I was hired to perform before the Barre Rotary Club children's holiday celebration, and then entertained at several local birthday parties with an "original" juggling and clown routine. And as icing on the cake, when I made the annual pilgrimage to the Bread and Puppet Circus up in Glover, Vermont, the following summer, I informally joined a group of amateur jugglers who were passing clubs, a new skill I had acquired after long hours of practice and lots of back strain from bending over to pick up dropped items during practice sessions.

Now, decades later, it is all a faded but cherished memory. Having reached the apex of my short circus career, I drifted to other compelling tasks like making a living, creating a relationship and life with Gabrielle, and raising my loving son Jamie. Happily, my career was proceeding well, and I was traveling to a dozen states, speaking and providing consultation. Gabrielle, too, moved on, taking a new position with Vermont's community college system.

Still, decades later, in the back corner of my upstairs clothes closet hangs my still colorful, if long-ignored, performance outfit, testifying to my more youthful days, my ambitions, and circus dreams that transformed into reality four decades ago.

A Good Eater

I know I have some bad habits and tendencies. Even though I have tried to keep them under wraps, some might have caught a glimpse of occasional self-centered behavior, pugnacious personality—not only in sports but in political work—and a vindictive streak that can stretch over the years. And like other New Yorkers, I have been noted as having a loud and expletive-laden vocabulary like the kind you might hear in a locker room.

However, one of my best traits is my lifelong habit of being a GOOD EATER, my one reliable skill. If you don't believe me, please consider the following.

Even in the most trying of circumstances such as relationships falling apart with drama and tears, the Red Sox fumbling a key play in the bottom of the ninth inning, losing my car keys, or misplacing my wallet, I am always very skilled at sitting down and devouring a good meal. Even with a pandemic knocking at our doors, I maintain a seat at the table: breakfast, lunch, and dinner. Believe me, not everyone can exhibit this skill. Can you?

In the 1960s, I was a student athlete at the University of Connecticut, where I played on the varsity basketball team. I lived in a dorm—Ethan Allen House—that had, among other virtues, a pleasant man named Al Bailey who was our dorm cook. Being a big sports fan, Al was more than ready to please, and I wish he were still alive to confirm that once a week on Hamburger Wednesdays, I was known to consume six burgers in a sitting. I still remember Al standing next to me as I finished up, with joy and satisfaction written all over his face, responding by saying, "Gosh!"

To further support my contention, I tell you that my interest in this subject remains focused and steady even in my golden years. To illustrate the point, I confess that my current reading priorities have shifted from my daily review of complex philosophical texts and comparative religious studies to a more pedestrian but no less important topic. I refer to my dedication to scouring, like a rabbinical scholar poring over a religious text, the Thursday *Times Argus* supplemental section with a colorful flyer from Shaw's supermarket. To confirm my vigorous and lifelong hearty appetite, I confess that I carefully study and examine the deals listed for the upcoming week. Forget for the moment the numbing effect of the pandemic and forget the challenges posed by my frugal nature. I have lust in my heart when I see that chicken drumsticks, thighs, or leg quarters are going for an astounding ninety-seven cents a pound. My eyes tear up when I see my beloved mussels listed for $2.99 a pound, a treat available to those who act quickly. I nearly stand and salute that I can express my patriotism and satisfy my appetite by buying one pound of deli meat and, in turn, getting a whole pound of American cheese for free. And to further strengthen my case for being an excellent hearty eater (I did not say politically correct or healthy eater; please give me some slack) I nearly swoon when noticing that, for $1.88, I can enjoy a Little Debbie chocolate snack box. At that price, I might make it two. Wouldn't you?

Just this morning, I made my way down the stairs to the kitchen in the early morning light. My heart was racing because today was an egg breakfast day. On that very morning, I started breakfast with the zeal and determination of an orchestra conductor. I led with some strong coffee and then listened for the nuanced sizzle of bacon on the stove. Whirling around, I pushed down the toaster after slicing my bagel, then cracked two eggs on the stove while flicking my wrist to pour a tall glass of orange juice. As the activity reached a crescendo, I grabbed my yogurt container and scooped a healthy amount into a bowl. And in honor of a recent tennis game or as an inducement to play better next time, I rewarded myself with a cookie or two as I drained my coffee mug.

As if further proof is needed, let me give you the final fact that proves that my good eating finesse has remained part of my core identity. Back in the 1950s, I was a student at Public School 114 in New York City. Classes were larger than we have in Vermont. I know because we were assigned seats based on a complex and approved scientific method called . . . seating by size places. Our seats were assigned according to our height. Naturally, the shortest kids got seats up front. That is why, in my sixth-grade class, I spent the entire year with a chair by the windowsill that served as my desk. Since our room was on the fifth floor, I had the best view of the beloved school playground, compared with having to turn to see our teacher up front.

As graduation approached, it was announced that every student would be recognized for their outstanding achievements. Not surprisingly, many of my classmates were asked to stand and be recognized for exceptional performance in English or reading, social studies, math, science, music, and even good penmanship. With each announcement, students received warm applause from parents in the audience. Finally, I heard my name called. The principal announced that I was also selected for recognition. With great pride, I tell you that I was the only student at P.S. 114 who received the GOOD EATER AWARD.

Adventures in Packwood, Washington

I picked up the ringing phone and recognized the voice immediately.

"What's wrong you don't call me anymore? I guess you are too busy for me. You just don't care," my mother added with voice rising, torturing me, picking away like a matador twirling a cape to enrage a bull. Before I could remind her that I had called her three days in a row, she complained in a shrill and amplified voice, "How come you never invite me on any of those exotic trips you take?"

It is essential to understand that my mom had a doctorate in a rare scientific field the title of which was Jewish Guilt. She had an innate, inborn talent for the subject, and she was a master at the practical application of this specialized science.

My mother had some tendency to exaggerate, not to mention to distort reality. I had rushed down to New York City not so many months ago to be by her side during an emergency. On that day, the caller had not been my mother but a city police sergeant who informed me over the phone that Lillian Libertoff had tried to commit suicide in her apartment and had been rushed to the psychiatric ward of a large New York City hospital. Dropping everything, I raced to the city and spent days by her bedside. As it turned out, it was not her first attempt or her last, but she recovered from each awful episode. I should know. I was a constant source of support during each hospitalization.

After fuming about her most recent call for a few days, I found some distance and perhaps balance. My mom was now eighty-four years old and a complex and challenging woman. We were close even if our relationship had many combustible parts, mixing love and affection, jealousies, criticisms, fits of anger, and her extreme mood swings, which drove her and everyone around her crazy. It did not escape me that at her age, she was still eager to travel. She had outlived most companions, so certainly, there were compelling factors that melted my initial anger at her disparaging and critical remarks. Besides, we were both in general agreement on political matters, leaning in a progressive direction, causing us to share a strong preference for the 2004 Democratic ticket with Howard Dean, former governor of Vermont and a rising star.

She was right about one thing. I did have ample opportunity to travel throughout the country and abroad. Speaking and consulting engagements alone had enabled me to visit more than thirty states, even Hawaii, during the past four years, and I had work assignments in France and South Africa. In more recent years, I had fallen in love with the northwest part of the United States, an attraction that was facilitated by various professional opportunities. I was particularly intrigued by Oregon and Washington states.

These states had received little notice or attention from me during my adolescent days. When I was a kid and avid baseball fan and the Brooklyn Dodgers took a "western trip," the team traveled to St. Louis and Cincinnati; the Northwest was not even on their radar nor mine.

On one of my first trips to Seattle, where I was speaking at a mental health conference, I spent four extra days exploring this unfamiliar region. I went into the deep backcountry like a natural roaming mountain man. My exact destination was uncertain, but I wanted to see and visit both Mount Rainier and Mount St. Helens, so I headed to that region. Unlike the renowned explorers of times past, I was "well armed" with a comfortable rented car and ammunition in my back pocket in the form of several credit cards.

When I first visited the area, I explored the region, and before settling on Packwood as a destination, I stopped in nearby Elba, Washington, to check out the Hobo Inn. I liked the eight caboose car rooms, but the cost was just north of eighty-five dollars a night. I considered that an expensive insult to hobos and to a particular explorer from the state of Vermont.

By chance and aided by luck, I found myself settling in the tiny, isolated village of Packwood, Washington. It had been love at first sight when I pulled into the small mountain town. Logging, hunting, and mining had defined the village high in the Cascade Mountains, a village that had seen better days. The spotted owl controversy had reduced logging operations in the region and gutted an already weak economy. The virtue of Packwood was its location, just outside of Mount Rainier National Park and near the back entrance of Mount St. Helens. It may have been isolated and economically depressed, but its natural setting was magnificent. I would go on to visit it during seven summers as I had frequent work assignments in Portland and Seattle. It was not always an easy ride. One mid-June when I departed Portland for a trip up to Packwood, my travels were thwarted by a road closure an hour south of Packwood because of massive snow piles in the Cascades. I had to retrace my steps, adding an extra three hours, and circle around to get to my destination.

A large chainsaw-carved sculpture of a bear sat in front of a two-story wooden log cabin building with a wraparound porch and a modest sign announcing the Hotel Packwood. If I'd had one, I would have tied my horse to the post in front of this "downtown" hotel. From my first visit, the owners, a married couple who looked like former loggers, welcomed me warmly and, at a later visit, confided that I was the best and probably only guest they ever had from Vermont. Besides the easy and enjoyable banter between us, the relationship was sealed with a most reasonable price of thirty-five dollars a night for a cozy room. The hotel had only eight rooms, and I felt comfortable in this homey, rustic setting with two pleasant communal bathrooms down the hall.

Besides, it did not take long to notice that some "locals" acted and dressed like characters out of a dime-store novel of Western culture. It was definitely "my kind of place."

Packwood had a hardly defined downtown and no traffic light, but its main thoroughfare offered a few stores. A rock shop, a saloon that could have been part of a western movie prop, two weather-beaten cafés, a tiny library open only on Tuesday and Thursday afternoons, and, of course, the Packwood Hotel were featured. I would be remiss if I didn't also mention the IGA grocery store, which was within walking distance. If you turned 180 degrees from its front door, the magnificent Mount Rainier—all 14,410 feet high—sat snowcapped and bright on sunny days, a view far better than any picture postcard could offer. Nearby, several boarded-up storefronts confirmed that Packwood was not a boomtown.

My next trip to the Northwest was a month or two away, and in one of those unscripted moments, I picked up the phone and called my mother. "Ma, it's me. How would you like to fly to Seattle, where I am speaking at a conference? Then we could drive out to the little town of Packwood near two national parks and explore for several days."

My mother was thrilled and uttered no derogatory or harmful words as I described the wonders of these two national parks. She was excited, but things turned abruptly when I told her more details about the accommodations at the Packwood Hotel. With laser focus, she responded quite negatively when I told her about the well-appointed communal bathrooms, one for men and one for women.

"You must be kidding me," she said. "I am not staying in a place without my own bathroom and shower," she emphatically informed me over the phone as we discussed the upcoming trip. When my mother was emphatic, she was a force to be reckoned with. Her mind could be like a steel trap slamming shut on an unfriendly idea like the shutting of a prison cell door.

That is how we pulled off the road just before reaching "downtown" Packwood after completing my work assignment in Seattle. Given my mom's refusal to stay at the Packwood Hotel, I had to be resourceful. I had little knowledge of alternative lodging opportunities in this area, so I dug into my home office desk drawer where I kept keepsakes from earlier visits. Relying on an old placemat from the Packwood Café, my favorite breakfast spot, I found an advertisement for a different motel, an alternative to the Packwood Hotel, a good three miles or so out of town.

I cannot recall the establishment's name, but it could have been the Twilight Motel or the Aging Badly Cottages. It probably had a one-star rating, but the advertisement highlighted an in-room phone and a bathroom complete with a shower. At the bottom of the ad, in small capital letters, was the dealmaker for me, "Breakfast included."

So it was that one late day in August my mom and I made our way towards this motel, seemingly the only dwelling in a forest of impressive old-growth trees. Pulling into the registration area, my mood was already slightly sour. This was because, when I'd booked the room the week before over the phone, the person on the other end had informed me that the daily tab was just under ninety bucks. Out of the side of my eye, I could see my mother intently gazing at the rather decrepit and beaten buildings. The frown on her face said it all, and her nose was bending out of shape at a frightening angle.

To be fair, my mother was a product of the bright lights of New York City and all of its trappings of trendy restaurants, upscale stores, beauty parlors, and elevator men at beck and call. For some reason, it galled me when my mother phoned and immediately quoted something from the *Times*, a paper she had read daily for decades, affecting a know-it-all, sometimes snotty, tone of urban sophistication with all the news that's fit to print. When necessary, or when I was in a cranky mood, I would undermine her by saying, "Mom, are you referring to the *New York Times* or the *Barre-Montpelier Times Argus,* our local paper, as your source?" She never thought this was as funny as I did.

I admit that the row of cabins spread out before us looked rather old and weathered. To say they were shabby wouldn't be an exaggeration, but I think it was more the fact that parked in front were five or six pickup trucks—all with at least one rifle in the gun racks behind the front cab, decorated with stickers ranging from scantily dressed women to Confederate flags—that set my mom's alarm system into a high pitch.

"I know this is one of your practical jokes, but it's not funny" was all my mother could muster in her indignant, no-nonsense voice. She made no effort to step outside of the car. "Stop playing games and take me to our lodging and let us have a nice dinner," she practically whimpered. "Besides," she added, "I'm dying to get the latest news about Howard," a prominent figure in our lives. I turned and smiled at her and nodded as I unlocked the car door and unpacked our luggage. Moving into this run-down motel complex with my mother was my immediate goal. Howard would have to wait. As my mother incorporated the reality of our situation, she reluctantly started to collect her pocketbook and one or two of her smaller bags. I sensed that she was stalling. "Mom, I wouldn't wait for the bellhop to come out and assist you," I sarcastically advised.

After getting the key at the main desk, I helped my mom walk to the cottage which had the number four on the door. The number four was a personal favorite of mine (worn by my childhood hero Duke Snider, centerfielder for the Brooklyn Dodgers back in the 1950s), but today, I suspected I needed more than a good luck charm. Upon opening the door, we were greeted by a décor that probably was in vogue early in the 1950s.

"Look, Mom," I said, "you should feel right at home." I patted several living room chairs and one huge couch, all encased in slightly faded plastic covers. "Why, the plastic coverings are just like I remember at Grandma's place in Brooklyn when I was a kid," I added for good measure. The windows were closed, rendering the room hot and stuffy with a stale scent. We sat for a minute to collect ourselves, but when we tried to get up, we both seemed to stick to the plastic as if an application of Elmer's Glue had been on the seat.

I laughed.

My mother frowned.

It wasn't that I was a neatnik like my mom, but I could tell that no one had cleaned or dusted the cabin in days or perhaps weeks. I found a dustpan in our kitchen closet, but searching for a broom was futile. I told my mom I would walk back to the main registration cabin for assistance. She seemed uneasy, and I heard her latch the door behind me as I departed. I had a flashback and remembered my mom taking me to see the movie *Psycho* when I was maybe thirteen and having her whimper in terror, practically hiding under the seat, to my great embarrassment. She did have a vivid imagination.

I quickened my pace, returned within minutes, bounded up the steps of our cabin, and knocked. Mom unlocked the door. "The cleaning crew is here. How can we help you?" I announced gaily and with cheer as I reentered the cabin.

At first, my mother showed disdain for our situation, but as we worked together, her attitude improved. The woman at the front desk had been accommodating although she looked overworked and underpaid. She had handed me not one but two brooms, which enabled my mom and me to be on the cleaning team together.

After a busy and productive thirty minutes, the place looked much improved, and so did my mother's mood. "Smile," I said as I clicked a picture on my little camera, capturing my mom with a broom in her hand, pants legs rolled up, and an overflowing dustpan. I mentioned with glee, "I bet you never stayed in a place like this." Unable to contain myself, I had to add, "I bet your snooty friends back in Manhattan will be impressed with this photo of a real mountain woman at work." At that moment, I thought I detected a smile.

It was close to six, and by some miracle, our tiny, old-fashioned TV with rabbit ears lit up when I turned the knob to "on" just as the Seattle station was preparing for the evening news report.

"I hope Howard had a good day," said my mom, who sat down on the couch with a squish of plastic announcing her arrival. Although Howard was not a member of our family, at that time, he was revered by my mother and a topic of daily discussion for us.

Howard Dean fell somewhere between being an old friend of mine and being a frequent political and legislative ally. We had shared a table in the cafeteria of the Vermont State House in the early 1980s when neither of us knew many State House regulars. Howard was a first-term member of the House of Representatives, and I was a relatively new director of the Vermont Association for Mental Health. We were newcomers and strangers to each other, but we discovered many common interests with healthcare and mental health treatment issues as bonding subjects. Besides, we both seemed to relish worthy political battles, including some that seemed like lost causes.

Over the next two decades, our friendship and shared political experiences created a strong relationship that could and did survive some serious public disagreements on legislative matters.

He was Vermont's governor in 1997 when I led a successful campaign to pass a law that mandated coverage for mental health and substance abuse conditions equal to that of physical health insurance. It quickly became a national model.

On a beautiful June morning, the governor hosted a large bill signing reception in his impressive State House office to celebrate the nation's first mandated parity legislation. The room was full of legislators, advocates, various local and national media reporters, officials from Washington, DC—easily identified by their expensive-looking three-piece suits—and, most notably, at least to me, my proud mother.

As things began to wind down, Howard graciously came over to say hello and be introduced to my mom. He immediately engaged her in friendly conversation, capitalizing on his considerable warmth and charm, not to mention his boyish smile. His attention and good words made Mother a dedicated and supportive fan for life.

Now, in the summer of 2004, Howard was the improbable leading Democratic presidential candidate. My mother was an active champion of his campaign back home in the greater New York area with her cadre of like-minded friends of a certain age, all of whom seemed most impressed that she had met him in person. If you listened to her tell it, Howard Dean was practically her lifelong family friend. But, in our family, who could be critical of minor exaggerations?

Within the first few moments of the television news, the reporting turned to the Dean's campaign and mentioned a speech he gave to a packed university crowd in Wisconsin. Not only did this satisfy my mom, but it gave us license to focus on a different important topic—where to eat dinner. Given my past visits, I knew options were limited, especially if a gourmet meal or relaxed ambiance were important. To further complicate matters, I had seen a notice on the front page of the weekly local paper announcing that the best restaurant in town, a term loosely applied, was temporarily closed due to some undisclosed issue with the county health department. Rather than waste time reviewing other options, none of which would be up to my mother's standards, I made an executive decision. "Mom," I said, "how would you like to accompany me for dinner at the Blue Spruce Saloon in the very heart of downtown Packwood?" I added with a flourish, "The treat is on me."

My mother, who I suspected was famished, said OK and then disappeared to change her clothes and wash up. Besides wearing a stylish skirt and clean blouse, she applied the usual overdose of perfume. She added some unnecessary jewelry that would have been perfect in a quaint little restaurant in Greenwich Village. More importantly, she carefully pinned a "Dean for President" button on her blouse. Months earlier, I had happily sent her an ample supply of Dean stickers and buttons, and I knew she always had a stash with her. I must admit the dark blue pin stood out smartly on her white shirt; Mom was back on her game, even if the Dean pin was oversized on her eighty-four-year-old frame.

After driving the three miles into town, we parked and headed for the Blue Spruce, a favorite of mine with its rough-and-tumble characters along with its western charm. As we approached the front door, the jukebox greeted us with loud country music. Mom's frowning face said it all. The saloon was not exactly her cup of tea.

Nevertheless, I took pleasure in guiding her into the saloon. It sported a large old-fashioned bar already populated by mustachioed cowboy types. They were attended to by a couple of young waitresses who sported their own cowboy hats and noticeably plunging necklines. In my opinion, the flashing neon "This Bud's For You" sign near the beer taps added some color and cheer. Several nearby pool tables were already busy with young and older men and women who hovered by the table to drink, laugh, smoke, and, God forbid, flirt.

Perhaps the place's ambiance slightly overwhelmed my mother or maybe it was her failing eyesight. Still, she didn't seem to notice that several men, in rather dark motorcycle attire and sporting shaggy beards, were chugging beers at an amazing rate. At the same time, smoke from cigarettes and joints bellowed out from their pool table den, creating nearly fog-like conditions. Certainly, the Blue Spruce Saloon was a far cry from and a contrast to those quiet, refined, and cozy dining establishments my mom was familiar with and favored in Manhattan.

The dinner proceeded better than I expected, helped perhaps

by the fact that my mom ordered a beer (a rare occurrence), which turned out to be a large Budweiser in a cowboy-sized glass, along with the Blue Spruce burger and fries. "How's the burger, Mom?" I asked in a loud voice, adjusting to her hearing challenges, which were, no doubt, further accentuated by a popular Willie Nelson tune blasting in the background.

"A little greasy," she replied. But, with relief, I noticed that she found comfort in the mound of French fries, a house specialty, which were disappearing at an impressive rate. The waitress came over, checking her hair and tugging on her miniskirt, to ask in a friendly manner if we needed anything.

"My mom would like another mug of beer," I replied with a mischievous smile. "Don't listen to him," my mother practically yelled, adding, "He's crazy, a real mashugana." This little banter ended abruptly since the waitress didn't know or understand Yiddish, but she seemingly got the drift. "Want anything else?" she asked again. Just minutes ago, my mom had told me she was "stuffed." Still, all this excitement must have activated her sweet tooth. She couldn't resist ordering a piece of chocolate cake for dessert and commanding that I help her "polish it off."

"That was lousy cake," my mother told me, in a voice loud enough for patrons at nearby tables to hear, as she scraped the last of the frosting off her plate, licking her fork clean on her now empty dessert dish. My contribution was one small helping as she attacked the cake with zeal. She left a dark chocolate smudge on her white shirt, which she did not notice until we returned to our cottage. I paid the bill with a flourish, and slowly, we made our way to the door.

I had parked the car up the street a block from the saloon so that Mom could get a better sense of the town's attractions. The rock shop stood out because the proprietor always had dozens of rocks on his sidewalk. My mother did not bother to respond when I told her this was the equivalent of window shopping on Fifth Avenue. I carefully guided her, aware that her gait and sight were compromised, and her noticeable unsteadiness was exacerbated by her consumption of one large draft beer.

It was still light out, and as we passed an open area with a small meadow and several trees, I warned my mom to be extra careful because there were some ornery characters up ahead. Clutching my arm, she slowed down. Sure enough, a mob appeared right near us in full dress, including some with strange trappings atop their heads.

It was a wild herd of giant elks, three or four dozen at least, residents of the surrounding mountains who had made their way down and were grazing in town on their frequent early summer evening strolls in Packwood. All my mom could say was, "I don't believe this," which she repeated several times.

This moment alone made the trip to Packwood worthwhile and gratifying. Besides, my mom and I had enjoyed the unique culinary highlights of the Blue Spruce Saloon, and now she agog over the elk, some with impressive antlers, who had invaded the town as we walked back to our rented car as the fading peaks of Mount Rainier served as a perfect backdrop.

Although my mom was always a fitful sleeper and an early riser, she snored at a steady clip when I opened my eyes the following day sometime before seven. I waited a half hour before I got out of bed and, with a bellowing voice, told my roommate, "Rise and shine," singing a verse or two of "Oh What a Beautiful Morning." It took her some time to get going, but she seemingly picked up speed when I enticed her with a reminder about the complimentary breakfast that awaited us. Being a big breakfast man, I wanted her to rush, but I knew this would be a slow process.

As I sat on the plastic-covered living room sofa, I could discern that old age and atrophy had significantly reduced my mother's stature and well-being. She had been a tall, more substantial woman filled with nervous energy just a few years ago. In light moments, I would joke with her in a caring, loving way. "Mom, if you could see, if you could hear, and if you could walk straight, you'd be almost perfect."

A shriek punctuated the morning silence. "I can't find my wallet," she wailed. Misplacing her wallet and keys was a lifelong affliction, and it was painful to watch her suffer. We both searched for her wallet in her bed and pocketbook. I found it. Somehow, Mom had dropped it behind the toilet. Slightly unsettled, we set off for breakfast. I noticed immediately that she was wearing her largest Dean campaign button. Given her reduced and now stooped body, the large Dean button almost looked like a type of body-battle shield, like armor worn by warriors in medieval days. I kept this thought to myself as we slowly walked from our cottage to the main office building and the promised "free" breakfast.

An unsettling scene greeted us in what might be called the breakfast dining room. Ten or eleven chairs were scattered around in an austere but modestly large area. No two chairs matched, but we settled into two oversized ones that were quite comfortable but noticeably worn and stained. I silently was thankful that my mom's eyesight was poor, and for once, she did not offer loud commentary. The fact that there were no tables was not an encouraging sign.

Most of the chairs were already filled with our cottage neighbors. Several middle-aged couples looked to be down on their luck and of the several rough-hewn men, at least two had apparently self-started their breakfast before ordering since several almost empty beer bottles sat in front of each of them. To my mild surprise, the chef and maître d' were none other than the couple who ran the motel cottage complex.

The kind, rugged woman who looked old beyond her years, the one who'd given me two brooms when I approached her in the registration area just yesterday, was now seated not next to a stove but to a hot plate while her husband, with pen and paper in hand, took orders. There was no written menu, but one could get eggs cooked to order and slices of greasy bacon with prepackaged muffins off to the side. The original advertisement for the place that caught my eye never said "fancy" complimentary breakfast!

"Could I see you outside?" I could tell from "that" tone and accompanying stare that Mother was not happy. I told our hosts and cottage mates that we would be right back, and she and I went outside. "I'm not eating here." That was not all she said. I only listened with half an ear and remembered words like pigsty, disgusting hot plate, drunks, and something about not even a table to eat on. "I will go to town on my own," she added.

Now it was my turn to get my back up. "Go ahead, Mom," I said. "Just go ahead and try to call a taxi in Packwood." "You might have better luck riding one of those large elk we saw last night," I added sarcastically.

Collecting myself, I modified my tone and attitude. "Mom," I said, "these folks mean well; they have a tough life, and remember, you were the one who insisted on a room with a private shower." And I added, unable to help myself, "Don't forget that our accommodations come with a complimentary breakfast, which is nothing to sneeze at."

I thought I caught a glimpse of a smile on my mother's lips when I mentioned the "free breakfast." "Besides," I added, using my well-honed lobbying skills to full advantage, "these are the very people you need to reach out to as a recruiter for Howard Dean in his presidential bid." I could feel my mother's resolve waver—running into town was not the thing to do—and feeling on a roll, I had to add, "Forget all those like-minded liberal Democratic friends back in Manhattan; Howard needs a broad coalition including the very folks waiting for breakfast inside our most modest cottage complex."

Returning to the breakfast setting, we were greeted by the smell of bacon as our hardworking chef slowly but carefully prepared individual meals on her small hot plate. Without enthusiasm, my mom ordered one scrambled egg and one piece of bacon and agreed to a cup of coffee, although I knew in advance that the watery-looking brew would go untouched. When I asked if she wanted a muffin in plastic wrap, my mother's face broke into a severe frown, and she shook her head "no." When it was my turn to order, I jokingly replied that, as an old lumberjack, three eggs with bacon on the side and a well-aged blueberry muffin would be mighty fine for me.

While my mom picked at her breakfast, I devoured my meal with relish. The coffee was weak, but the steaming cup matched well with my slightly stale but not unpleasant blueberry muffin. And it is hard to ruin scrambled eggs even when cooking on a hot plate.

The conversation was limited, but someone tried to make small talk and asked us where we were from. Then one of the early morning drinkers, the one who had just opened another bottle of brew, said to my mother, "What's that on your button?" I assume that this gent suffered not only from a possible drinking problem but from some deficiency in his eyesight; the button was indeed oversized, and the name Dean stood out nicely. The inquiry alone caused everyone to look up and turn toward my momentarily embarrassed mom.

"It's a Dean for President button, and I am working on his campaign." Her announcement was greeted with . . . silence. To support my mom, I jumped in and indicated that I, too, was a fan and backer, leaning over and taking a button from my mom's purse where she kept her campaign stash. Bravely, she asked if anyone would like a campaign button. There was no response just an uneasy silence. Our breakfast gathering was coming to a close.

"Nothing ventured, nothing gained," I whispered to my mom as the breakfast crowd shuffled out. Then, in one of those defining moments, the woman who ran the front desk and who had served us breakfast came over and asked if she could have one of the Dean buttons. She spoke in hushed tones, mentioning that Packwood was really conservative, and people there hated Dean. I wish you could have seen my mother's face as she fished in her purse and picked out an attractive campaign button. Mom's face was flushed with excitement and satisfaction. She reached out and hugged the woman. I felt that she was feeling useful and accomplished as she announced that Howard Dean would get at least one vote in Packwood thanks to her.

Over the next two days, I gave my mother a guided tour of Mount St. Helens park and then a carefully constructed visit to the expansive Mount Rainier area. I drove her as close as possible to most spots because we were high in the mountains, and my mother's breathing was noticeably labored. Although I had some reserve about stressing my mom, I enthusiastically guided her on a special mile-long walk in the Grove of the Patriarchs, a forest of old-growth trees, some more than one thousand years old. I know I pushed my mother on this trek, but this walk was a ritual with me on every visit. We both looked up in awe at the massive Douglas firs, hemlocks, and cedars, some of which were more than three hundred feet tall. This hike was indeed one of my better presents to my mother.

When I look at the photograph of us—me in a favorite red Hawaiian shirt; mom next to me, smartly dressed with a small campaign pin on her blouse; Howard Dean, with us in spirit if not in person during his improbable presidential campaign; and Mount Rainier towering above us, snowcapped and handsome—it brings back favorite memories. These memories are made all the more special because this trip would prove to be our last long-haul adventure together. The ravages of old age, as well as the trouble she had walking, breathing, seeing, and hearing, were very real barriers for my mom, and perhaps I, too, felt challenged in the role of the lone guide and caretaker.

It gave me great pleasure to remind her in the years to follow that she was, among other things, a successful political activist.

"Mom," I would say," "you were Howard Dean's number one best recruiter and advocate in Packwood, Washington, during the entire 2004 presidential campaign."

This recollection never failed to bring a smile to her face until the very day in February 2016 when she died at age ninety-five.

Thinking about Ralph Geer

Ralph Geer, a man of few words, communicated not with long, elegant sentences but with hammers, drills, saws, paint brushes, chain saws, shovels, and ladders. Whether a job was big or small, he exhibited a sense of purpose and pride in all he did.

At first, his name appeared on my refrigerator list of helpers—plumbers, electricians, and emergency utility numbers. Over three decades, Ralph's name rose to the top as a reliable, skilled craftsman and also as a person I bonded with in admiration and mutual respect.

In September, my wife, Sarah, and I returned from a bike trip out west. It took a couple of days to get settled, but Ralph was high on my list of people to call—not because I needed his help but because he might need mine.

A few months earlier, Ralph had shared the news that he had been diagnosed with lung cancer. I had been stunned, surprised, and upset for him. Trying to boost his spirits, I'd related stories about friends who had successfully battled major health problems. Ralph seemed unmoved and almost resigned. Perhaps he best understood his dire prognosis. He was not one to talk about his feelings or, for that matter, ask for help. I struggled too as I tried to figure out how to be a supportive friend when devastating news was close at hand. Already, Ralph was experiencing the side effects of chemotherapy; he was weak and slightly unsteady.

I asked Ralph if I could prepare and bring over meals to his house in Calais. He showed little enthusiasm; that is, until I reminded him how much he'd enjoyed a meatloaf sandwich I'd made him while he'd been working on a back porch project.

His eyes brightened, and he consented. He recalled enjoying the sandwich and remembered that the recipe came from my mother. Over the next couple of months, I prepared meatloaf meals, then raced to his house in order to deliver a warm dinner. The day before I departed for Wyoming, I promised Ralph another "meatloaf special" upon my return. He gave me one of his rare smiles.

As it turned out, I was late by a couple of days. Ralph Geer died just as I returned from the trip out west.

Until his illness, although slightly built, he had been a vigorous and powerful man. His death at age sixty-nine came too early. It was probably of little consequence that he did not get to enjoy one more meatloaf dinner, but I lamented that he missed this particularly glorious foliage season by a couple of weeks. Ralph reveled in Vermont's fall colors and the wonder of our transition from summer to deep fall.

We were a strange pair. My lack of mechanical aptitude and building skills, while not legendary, were obvious to family, to friends, and to Ralph. I sat in awe of his knowledge and skills. He could tackle any mechanical problem, construction project, or repair project. The more complex the project, the more Ralph rose to the occasion, always coming through in the clutch like one of his beloved Red Sox players.

Ralph was shy, unassuming, and independent. In thirty years of projects at the house, Ralph never engaged with a partner or assistant. Only rarely would he ask for help moving some heavy object. We often ate lunch together during the noon hour. Ralph said little, but he seemed to relish my stories and banter.

Since Ralph's passing, Sarah and I cannot go a day without paying homage to this sweet and gentle man. Ralph, years ago, working alone, installed a beautiful blue metal roof atop our house, laid a wood floor in the kitchen, built steps out front, fixed countless doorknobs, replaced an ugly and very old linoleum floor, and remade a study for Sarah. He was exacting in his work and had a natural eye for practical, cost-effective improvements.

A few years ago, Sarah planned a birthday party for me on Sparrow Farm Road, rounding up the usual suspects—family, friends, and neighbors—for an evening of celebration. I added Ralph to the guest list. Not only did I consider him a friend, but he was an integral part of the very house I had lived in for more than four decades. My only hesitation was that I knew hanging out in a crowded living room with strangers would not be his idea of a good time.

On a mid-January day with glorious fluffy snow and crisp cold air, the house filled with spirited conversation. The only person missing was Ralph. Just as we served the food, I heard a knock on the side porch door. Ralph stood there, a mantle of white on his winter cap, and apologized for being late. I told him how pleased I was that he had come.

I ushered Ralph in and found an empty seat near the wood stove. The next hour was filled with food, storytelling, cake, and song. Ralph was quiet, but I could see from across the room that to my relief, several people chatted with him.

As the evening ended, one by one and in couples, people made for the exit with final words, hugs, and kisses. Several friends needed assistance, so I walked them out to their parked cars along the snowy road. When I returned, I was surprised to find Ralph the last person remaining. It was, for me, a joyful moment.

In his quiet way, Ralph told me he appreciated being invited and said he had a good time. For him, this might be considered an extensive, personal conversation. His eyes shifted down under his chair, and he pulled out a wrapped parcel. "Happy birthday," he said and handed me the package.

This may have been my very best birthday present: a pair of Carhartt work gloves given in friendship and with affection.

Playing Out the Clock

As my graduation approached in the spring of 1966, I realized I would never again experience the thrill of being on the basketball court in the electric environment of the old, packed fieldhouse at the University of Connecticut. During my undergraduate tenure from 1962 to 1966, the old fieldhouse gym had attracted boisterous, overflowing crowds of loyal Husky fans. It was *the* place to be on a cold winter night.

I proudly wore my Connecticut uniform with short shorts, high socks, and the number 34 on my jersey top, prancing in warm-ups as the pep band hammered out the stirring UConn Husky fight song. Almost six decades later, I can close my eyes, feel the energy, and hear the spirited refrain. It remains prominently embedded in my "memory bank."

These were prosperous years for UConn basketball. During my three varsity years, the Huskies were Yankee Conference champions. Evidence of this achievement sits in my old Vermont farmhouse in the form of a small silver bowl marking our victorious tenure. One highlight still celebrated with a banner hanging in the newer, larger Harry A. Gampel Pavilion at UConn, was our success in 1964 when we progressed to the Elite Eight in the NCAA basketball tournament. Our "Cinderella season" ended when we played and lost to Duke University. Nevertheless, a thousand fans turned up at Bradley International Airport outside of Hartford to escort us back to the Storrs campus as part of a raucous celebration that lasted well into the night.

I remained wedded to the sport and proudly "played out the clock" in the decades to come with various teams on courts near and far. Throughout the ages, I played with passion, joy, and appreciation for teammates. I wasn't a star but a consistent role player at UConn. While specific moments on the court fade like sunlight behind thickening clouds, there is gratitude for the common bond and camaraderie in the ebb and flow of basketball action enhanced greatly by our success on the hardwood courts in the mid-1960s.

I continued my postcollege basketball career, playing competitively until my fiftieth year. During that time, I happily associated with "local" teams, tracing my path through life in various New England communities.

During those years, I also played in countless pickup games on courts from New York City to the far West. Despite regional differences, whether on the asphalt courts on West 4th Street in Greenwich Village or under the spiffy, well-tended hoops in Berkeley, California, near the university, there was a sense of community and a bond connecting those who played. Despite intense competitiveness along with class, social, and racial differences that at times ratcheted up tension and strife, there prevailed a culture of respect for anyone—regardless of race, economic status, or ethnic background—who could "find the open man," crash the boards, box out on a rebound, and, most importantly, hit a long-range jumper to break a tie score.

Nearly sixty years have passed since 1966, and I still relish the memory of playing on several teams that afforded countless opportunities for challenge, anticipation, and the perpetuation of hoop dreams. In different gyms across New England, the sights, sounds, and fragrance of "league games" have remained part of my DNA. Being on the winning end was always uplifting while a defeat carried disappointment. It is challenging to remember specific outcomes but easy to appreciate those special moments that featured teamwork, high fives, and the sense of pulling together as a unit. Moments of discord, trash-talking, and not-so-gentle shoving seem like minor disturbances when compared to the many times of passionate bonding on the hardwood floors.

Two years after graduating in 1968, I settled in New Haven, Connecticut. It wasn't long before I was invited to play in the YMCA basketball league, which was highly competitive. New Haven schools were a hotbed of basketball rivalry, and Hillhouse and Wilbur Cross High School graduates comprised the lineups of many league teams. My team, the New Haven Truckers, was composed of a diversified group including several outstanding local Black players who graduated from the inner-city schools and several experienced former East Haven High School standouts from the city's Italian community. I was the outsider but fit in well with my jump shot and an expansive Afro hairdo topped with massive curls. Our team was outstanding. In 1969, the Truckers won the YMCA city league championship. We started the season slowly, but once we all accepted that there was only one basketball and five excellent shooters, we learned to share the scoring load and successfully made our way through an intense season.

During that time, I was a regular at the YMCA gym and made new friendships, which were meaningful to a relative newcomer. I developed a special bond with my locker mate, Mike Katz. On occasion, Mike needed my help lacing his sneakers. Mike was a little stiff and noticeably muscle-bound. Mr. Katz, you see, was the reigning Mr. America. He was humble and pleasant in our locker-room conversations, and it could be said that my assistance helped him retain his bodybuilding crown for a couple of years. He would eventually lose that distinction to a much more dynamic young fellow from Austria named Arnold Schwarzenegger, who, I believe, was able to tie his sneaker laces without assistance.

After the 1969 championship basketball game, in a moment of reckless abandon, I suggested that our team gather for a victory party the following night at my place on 241 Lawrence Street. Everyone showed up, but America in 1969 was tumultuous. A celebratory evening soon transformed into a minor disaster when after finishing a keg of beer, we turned the conversation to the raging Vietnam War and the emerging notoriety of the highly controversial Black Panther Party. The divergent views of various players boiled over with voices rising. The gathering ended when two slightly inebriated "war hawks," young white men from East Haven, left in a huff, slamming the downstairs side porch door as they departed. My other teammates quickly finished their beers and drifted off with discord and division polluting the air. Our political differences off the court were reflective of the tenor of the country. A group of diverse guys who bonded over basketball on the league-champion Truckers team had no defense when a social situation gave us a chance to discuss divisive issues like Vietnam and race relations.

A couple of years later, my wife and I moved to Cambridge, Massachusetts, as I began my first year in graduate school at Harvard University in 1971. Like a magnet, I was drawn to Harvard's Briggs Athletic Center on the second floor of a majestic building on campus. My friend and academic professor, Ira Goldenberg, a Bronx product who resembled actor Al Pacino both in persona and speech, knew the city game and fancied himself—with reason—a crafty and competent playmaker and a reliable point guard. He often set me up for an easy two-pointer or layup. Professor Goldenberg took great delight in our three-on-three matchups, and when we won, he walked around with a crooked smile all afternoon. With mutual instincts and nonverbal communication, we bonded beautifully on the court. Off the court, he was the person who saw something in me that motivated him to lift me and give me confidence and opportunity. His intense personality, sense of humor, and insightful, sharp mind made him an actual role model.

Several years later, one of the lunchtime players asked me if I would be interested in playing in the Harvard Graduate School League. It did not take much convincing, and in 1974 and 1975, I was starting as a forward on the Long Balls—one of the more creative team names in the popular graduate league. The level of play was competitive but below that of the YMCA in New Haven.

Playing in that graduate league allowed me to meet interesting and talented guys. One highlight of my first season occurred right after our first game, which we won by three points. The organizer of our Long Balls team was a pleasant graduate student named William Farragut III. As we celebrated our victory, it was suggested that we organize several practice sessions. William followed up and started asking each player for a home telephone number. Since we were in the steamy bathhouse section, showering, the timing seemed odd to me. In what I would characterize as a remarkable performance, he listened as players rattled off their phone numbers, and he put them into his memory bank. William, you see, had a photographic memory. This performance in the shower was more impressive than any no-look behind-the-back pass on a fast break!

During the summer of 1974, I spent the month of July on the beautiful island of Martha's Vineyard. One day after I arrived, I read an article in the *Vineyard Gazette* that detailed the schedule for the island's summer league basketball season. I called the number listed for additional information, and by the end of the conversation, because of my background and experience, I was assigned to the Martha's Vineyard Bulls. Two days later, I drove down to the town of Oak Bluffs for our first game on an outdoor court sporting several rows of benches and lights for the evening games.

After spending many days that summer down on Zack's (bathing suit optional) Beach in Gay Head, the westernmost town on the island, it was a pleasure to play outdoors in the cooling evening air with fans cheering from the stands. When the pace picked up, I can recall wiping salty sweat from my eyes, a gesture that reminded me of swimming and bodysurfing in the ocean hours earlier that day. The daily afterglow from mixing the warm summer sun, the lingering ocean air, and the rhythmic sound of the basketball on the Oak Bluffs court was nothing short of a sensual delight.

There was one other summer resident who lived on Center Road in Chilmark and who played on the Vineyard Bulls team. He was younger than me by three years and played basketball for Dartmouth College. We had common interests, and I was impressed when I learned that his father was a writer of considerable fame. He and I decided to carpool to games together, and I transported him in my old, much beloved Saab automobile. Shaped more like a fat cigar, it had a large sunroof, and it served us well as we made the return evening trips home, usually stopping first for a beer in the Ritz Café along the main drag in Oak Bluffs. As the cool air dried our still-damp bodies, we headed west toward Chilmark. Still energized by our recent basketball game, and buoyed by the ice-cold beer, our spirits soared. Like two teenagers, we sang together—accompanied by my rather tinny Saab radio—songs like "American Pie" as we made our way home on the dark, winding roads. These were joyful days and nights.

In 1975, as I neared completion of my coursework at Harvard and began preliminary work on my dissertation, we moved to Annisquam, a beautiful section of Gloucester on the north shore of Massachusetts. Through contacts in the graduate school program, I learned of a house-sitting opportunity in this old seaport village, beginning in the early fall and running through the following spring. The colonial house was lovely with a pleasantly large bedroom and a smaller space—perfect for a soon-to-arrive baby. Adding to the joy, the beach was just a short walk away, and the old, charming Annisquam library was just minutes away on foot. Son Jamie was born on February 18, 1976, and spent his first months in this lovely neighborhood.

Moving to the North Shore gave me another basketball opportunity, and I found myself recruited to play in the winter Gloucester Basketball League. The level of play was modest, but the primarily blue-collar participants showed enthusiasm and grit. My team, the Gloucester Sharks, was composed of young men who were full-time fishermen from the busy port downtown. They were good guys, hardworking and fun-loving. And what they lacked in basketball skills, they made up for in effort and attitude. Our team did well in league play, and after our second game, we retired to a bar called Captain Courageous to share some social time. I was ever so impressed by their "fish tales" and the challenges associated with making a living from the sea.

I had little to add or to compare to their stories. In my entire life, I had only fished once, when I was a kid in Rockaway, and I managed to pull in some clumps of not-very-impressive seaweed. I did mention that I had just discovered a new favorite seafood delight, a shellfish known as steamers. Imagine my surprise when after our next game ended, one of my friendly teammates asked me to join him at his truck parked outside the gym. Inside the backseat was a modest-sized garbage can. It was filled with steamer clams! For the rest of the season, my teammates took turns in bringing big containers of fresh steamers, which were as tasty as they were plentiful. To this day, I cannot eat this seafood favorite without thinking about my Gloucester teammates' generous friendship and camaraderie.

Basketball played a special, if peculiar, role in my decision to move to Montpelier, Vermont, in 1976. At the time, I was writing my dissertation to complete my doctoral degree, and there was no reason to stay in Massachusetts. Several factors propelled this move. To begin with, we had to vacate the Annisquam house as the summer approached, making way for the owners who were now eager to enjoy their summer vacation home. On a practical level, finding new lodgings in Cambridge with an infant in tow would be challenging and expensive. More importantly, I sensed that if I stayed in or around Boston, I would live my entire life in an urban environment. Vermont, which had become a beacon and magnet for the countercultural movement, had considerable appeal.

Besides, while at UConn, I had made three long bus trips to Burlington, Vermont, when snowstorms canceled flights as we competed against the University of Vermont Catamounts. On two of these long bus trips, I successfully secured a front bus seat and was positioned to embrace the overwhelming beauty of the countryside as we made our way north. The interstate was yet to be built, so as we entered the Green Mountain State, we passed one small snowy village after another on winding, hilly roads marked by pastures and forests mantled with white. While we traveled on the western side of the state and nowhere near Montpelier, the ambiance and beauty of the scenery made a most favorable and romantic impression, one that would have a considerable impact in the coming years.

My last road trip to the University of Vermont was in 1966. Ten years later, as I sat in Annisquam, I opened the Sunday *Boston Globe* and found the classified employment section. Resolved to explore some new directions, I was drawn to a job offering in the Vermont listings. An organization called the Washington County Youth Service Bureau, based in Montpelier, was looking for an executive director. Considering my work with children in New Haven and Boston and extensive contacts nationally, a position in a youth services organization sounded like a natural fit. I had never been to Montpelier, but its French-sounding name was alluring.

I typed up an application letter on my manual typewriter, updated my resume, and entered the job market. To my surprise, I received an immediate response, and an interview was scheduled. On a mid-March morning, I pulled out of the driveway in Annisquam—which already had a few early flowers peeking out in front—encouraged by the moderate weather of the nearby ocean. My interview was scheduled for midafternoon, and as I turned north, I was uncertain about the wisdom of moving so quickly and perhaps scared of venturing to points unknown. I knew no one in Vermont and not much about the state and its rural culture. Little did I know I was heading on a trip that would change the direction of my life.

What started as a pleasant morning in Annisquam changed when I hit White River Junction on the New Hampshire–Vermont border. As I focused on the "Welcome to Vermont" sign, I noticed graceful snowflakes swirling in the air. Ten miles further north, the gentle flakes had turned into what seemed to me a blizzard. Reaching Randolph, I had to strain to make out the outline of the beautiful Green Mountains, which followed the highway toward Montpelier. In this winter wonderland, I exited at the Montpelier sign. As I drove into town, I was immediately attracted to the handsome State House and the charm of the old but most attractive buildings that straddled Main and State streets. A foot of fresh snow graced the capital city.

My interview was successful and engaging. The staff seemed committed and reflected the values and tone of Vermont's countercultural community, not to mention the dress and appearance of a vibrant alternative, hippie culture. The actual hiring process that unfolded became nothing short of a saga. The staff supported my candidacy while the board was inclined to select an older, more experienced candidate. The board announced their choice, selecting the veteran administrator. Within days, the Youth Bureau staff revolted, and everyone threatened to quit the organization unless I was offered the position.

The turn of events unsettled me. My primary staff contact at the Youth Service Bureau, a dedicated, charming, and energetic woman named Claudia Jacobs, called me several times a day during that fateful week, imploring me to stay tuned and committed. Already, she was detecting reservations on my part. Given all the changes, I was having second thoughts.

This was my first foray into seeking a full-time job since starting graduate school. Deciding to pick up and leave a familiar urban environment with an infant son was daunting and overwhelming.

And there were references to rural culture that had me fazed, like heating with wood and dealing with blizzards and extreme cold, not to mention something called "mud season."

Claudia called and informed me that on the following day, the Youth Service Bureau board chairperson would call and offer me the head job. Now my fears and doubts intensified. After giving her a list of possible problems and barriers to this move and a final decision, I added, perhaps grasping for more time, that it was unlikely that in a small town like Montpelier, there would be any basketball presence, and the sport was essential to my physical and mental health.

Early the following day, hours before I heard from the board chair, Claudia called and informed me with enthusiasm that she had signed me up for the Montpelier Men's Basketball League. How could I say no? An hour later, I formally accepted the job on a phone call with the board's chairperson.

Over the years, I spent many hours at the Barre Street gym, playing in the Montpelier basketball league and at noontime pickup basketball games on Monday, Wednesday, and Friday. I played for several league teams, including Miller's Concrete and Carriveau's Gulf Station. The level of play was uneven but intense. Games were rough-and-tumble affairs, as were many team participants. Yet entering the gym on a winter night never lost its thrill, and as an added highlight, I brought young Jamie to games even if they ended way past his bedtime. Seeing my young son watching every move and cheering me on greatly pleased me. Recalling individual games is challenging, but the *Times Argus* did have summary reports, and this was indeed community basketball, bonding players throughout central Vermont in a basketball fraternity.

A diverse group of players showed up at the gym for intense noon pickup basketball games. If you won, you stayed on the court, but if you lost, you were banished to the bench and waited until space opened. Some players showed up as early as 11:45

A.M. since it increased the likelihood of being selected for the first contest. Games were five-on-five affairs with winners securing seven baskets. As we approached one o'clock, the most common refrain was "just one more game." It seemed like grown men were almost magically transformed into young boys despite expanding waistlines and receding hairlines.

It should be noted that in 1986, a young woman named Kathy Johnson added diversity and her considerable skills as a league and noontime player. More than a few male players had trouble matching her skill level.

At age fifty, I hung up my sneakers. It was not a highlight film ending, but the story has richness and drama. I was engaged in an informal pickup game at lunchtime. One player that day, a man of considerable size and weight, was challenged not only by age and slowing reflexes but with a terrible temper. On this day, he was guarding me tightly, but I gave him a fake to the left; he fell for it and stumbled. I went right for an easy basket. This was not unusual, but for some reason, this man, a lawyer in town, "lost it." Enraged, he came up to me yelling and kicked me hard in the hip without further comment. I was stunned and in pain. In the heat of a game, an occasional push or shove was viewed as poor behavior but not unknown. A hard kick in anger was dangerous and unacceptable.

My swift reaction was appropriate for a man of fifty who grew up on the basketball courts in Rockaway. I jumped on him, knocked him to the ground, and got in some well-placed punches as he retaliated. The other players separated us where we were rolling on the floor and restored some semblance of order, but the damage had been done.

Leaving the gym after showering, I limped to the State House, where I was scheduled to testify in the early afternoon. In a most unusual moment, the chair of the Vermont Senate's Appropriations Committee paused the hearing, calling a short recess so that I might have an opportunity to wash my face since blood from a cut above my right eye was dripping onto my written testimony. I completed my presentation with a wet cloth applied to my wound.

When I sat at home that evening with an ice pack on my throbbing thigh and a cold, damp washcloth dabbing at my now noticeable black eye, I decided it was time to retire from the game I loved.

Weeks later, I walked out on the second-floor landing of my downtown office at 43 State Street. Someone from the third floor was approaching, a pleasant woman with a tennis racquet over one shoulder. We chatted briefly, and then Elaine Alfano asked if I would like to hit some balls with her down at the Montpelier Recreation Field later that week. I hesitated initially since I had never seriously played the game, but I decided to try it. This decision helped my transition from basketball while enabling me to discover a new athletic passion. On that first day of tennis with Elaine, I struggled to keep the ball in play and over the net. Little did I know that Elaine would become a good friend and frequent doubles tennis partner for two decades.

When I pass the old gym on Barre Street, which even in its heyday would not be confused with the regal basketball palace, Madison Square Garden in New York City, I recall many beautiful moments. Most people might pass the gym and see nothing but an old, tired building soon to be closed, perhaps converted into a small apartment complex. I see it and think: here is an enchanted magical place where I and many others experienced the simple passion for a beautiful game.

Ode to Jim Jeffords

It was a rousing and memorable start to a new millennium.

On May 18, 2000, I sat front and center in an overflowing, ornate US Senate Conference Hearing Room on Capitol Hill, awaiting my turn to testify before the Senate Committee on Health, Education, Labor, and Pensions (HELP). As the gavel announced the session's opening, chairperson Senator Jim Jeffords welcomed the overflow crowd. Sitting on the dais were significant proponents of the bill on mental health parity legislation to be considered, including Senators Paul Wellstone (D-Minnesota) and Peter Domenici (R-New Mexico). Senator Ted Kennedy (D-Massachusetts), another supporter of Bill S.796, sat next to Wellstone. The remaining members filled out the seats and looked out over the audience.

Several years earlier, in 1997, Vermont had passed the nation's most comprehensive mental health parity legislation model. Governor Howard Dean had signaled his support in a full-blown bill signing ceremony in his Vermont State House office in Montpelier on a beautiful June day.

When I reviewed a draft of the federal legislation, I found it lacking. The proposed bill only recommended parity for some severe mental health conditions and fell far short of being comprehensive. In addition to failing to cover any childhood conditions, it lacked the power of being a mandated benefit.

I had an opportunity to meet with Senator Jeffords earlier in the year in his Montpelier office to discuss and highlight these critical shortcomings. In past years, we had had other occasions to discuss policy issues, but this conversation was of greater significance. As a key Republican and chair of a powerful committee, Senator Jeffords was upfront with me about the favorable prospects of this proposed bill. There was already a formidable list of backers, including the outspoken liberal Senator Wellstone and the staunch conservative Senator Domenici. While Senator Jeffords remained silent on his position on this specific proposal, he confirmed his desire to improve access to mental health treatment.

Senator Jeffords was not an eloquent or animated speaker but a good listener. To my surprise, we spent an entire hour discussing the proposed legislation. He inquired about Vermont's bill and how it differed from the federal legislation under consideration. He ended the meeting by saying that he would give it some additional thought, but as we shook hands, it was clear to both of us that my possible testimony would create a stir and upset the momentum in favor of the proposed federal bill. I did not anticipate being invited to address the HELP committee.

A week later, Senator Jeffords's office called and told me I had been added to the list to testify in the upcoming Senate hearing.

I flew down to Washington, DC, in advance of the hearing, making sure I would have time to finalize my testimony. Early on the day of the hearing, I had my usual hearty breakfast, showered, and dressed in my cleanest shirt and dress jacket. Although I was most familiar with the metro train system in Washington, I celebrated this special occasion by taking a cab to Capitol Hill. I paid the cabbie and added a generous tip. I was both excited and nervous. By design, I arrived an hour prior to the hearing.

More than a month earlier, I had rejected an offer from my parent organization, the National Mental Health Association, to have them prepare my written remarks. Taking umbrage at their attempt to control the substance and tone of my position, I drafted my testimony at home using pen and paper.

As I walked down the corridor of the Senate building, I was surprised, actually shocked, to see a vast crowd gathered already, probably a hundred people in a line outside the meeting room entrance. It was a young crowd, and many were dressed informally, looking like college students lounging on a Sunday morning. Confused, I checked my notes to see if I had the wrong location. Confirming my information, I approached two Senate guards responsible for keeping order out in the hall. They explained that when issues of particular interest were scheduled, it was standard practice for many organizations and lobbyists to hire "stand-ins." This procedure allowed chief executives and industry leaders to arrive just minutes before the hearing and secure well-placed, guaranteed seats. To a Vermont resident, this seemed excessive and clearly a power play, and it reminded me that I was on a steep learning curve about protocols at our nation's capital. It left me feeling unsettled and missing the more informal, friendly environment of the Montpelier State House, where everyone had equal status when attending committee hearings.

When I was ushered in fifteen minutes before the hearing, I was escorted by an official guard, a sturdy middle-aged man dressed in formal attire and sporting a communications device in his left ear. As I settled into my seat, I took notice of the large, magnificent, and imposing room and the fact that some audience members were standing along the side walls. The room was filled and then some.

The committee members were elevated, looking lordly and talking to each other with animation. Seated below them but slightly above the audience were those who were invited to testify. I was ushered to sit in this section. The room resonated with a certain "buzz," reminding me of the minutes before the opening tip-off of a college basketball game, although cheerleaders and a pep band were absent.

As anticipated, the first eleven witnesses spoke favorably of the proposed bill. The list included the National Institute of Mental Health's director, several national advocacy groups, and the American Psychiatric Association. There was even a strong endorsement from industry in the form of Delta Airlines. The next speaker, representing the Health Insurance Association of America, read a bland statement that argued that this bill would raise insurance rates without publicly opposing the proposed legislation.

I was the thirtieth and last person to testify. Senator Jeffords took the initiative to introduce me and requested that I explain the content and scope of Vermont's parity bill. As I completed this first part of my commentary, Senator Kennedy responded with a statement, not a question. "We passed a similar bill in Massachusetts a year ago," he crowed, looking more than a little pleased.

Now it was my turn to respond. "With all due respect, Senator Kennedy, the Massachusetts bill lacks a mandate." This allowed the insurance industry in the Commonwealth to offer optional mental health coverage in many health policies as well as to charge higher and even exorbitant fees. "The Massachusetts approach," I added with my voice rising, "is not parity." My comment caused some buzz in the audience. Senator Jeffords gaveled for silence and asked me to proceed.

Gaining confidence, I stated that the concept behind this bill should be to equalize coverage for mental health and substance abuse. I argued that this bill should be considered a civil rights fight and an attempt at insurance fairness. Viewed from that perspective, I further stated that the proposed legislation, S. 796, fell far short of being a significant proposal. For the next ten minutes, I exposed the federal proposal as a piecemeal approach, far short of the comprehensive parity legislation adopted by the state of Vermont. I ended my presentation with a flourish, "Anything less than full parity is partial discrimination!"

My critical comments caused an immediate reaction. Senator Kennedy stated his strong support for the bill, as did committee member Chris Dodd, and Peter Dominici, one of the two cosponsors. The other cosponsor, liberal lion Paul Wellstone, took me to task for my unwillingness to compromise. Several other members of the committee stated their support for the bill.

Senator Jeffords stepped in and announced that all comments would be recorded for the record, but he did not allow me to respond further. However, Senator Wellstone interjected and, in an unusual move and one that challenged protocol, asked the chair to invite me back to the microphone. Senator Jeffords agreed and had me return to the witness table.

Since I had already been the one and only witness to state opposition to the bill, calling me back to testify further raised the stakes. I sensed that if a vote were taken, there would be support for the proposed parity bill in the HELP committee. Having me testify a second time created further tension in the room, and Senator Wellstone immediately laced into me and my earlier testimony. His simplified argument was that something was better than nothing and that his bill would achieve parity coverage for many Americans. He was livid.

I reviewed my opposition step-by-step. It summarized all the arguments I had shared with Senator Jeffords. It would be accurate to say that Senator Wellstone was furious. He ended our heated exchange by asking me point blank whether his legislation (cosponsored with Senator Domenici) was an important step forward. The audience was dead silent; one could hear a pin drop. I replied without flinching, stating that for all intents and purposes, the legislation would be a step "sideways."

What happened next, I will never forget. Chaos erupted, and the sedate decorum of the Senate room was momentarily absent. Some in the audience offered loud, critical comments while many stood and applauded my position.

Chairperson Jeffords gaveled the room to order. In summary fashion, he terminated the hearing. The crowd slowly dispersed, not without expressions of heated emotion on both sides of the issue. Senator Wellstone's key policy staff member was furious. She voiced her opinion of my action in language most heated with phrases not uncommon to locker-room talk.

Through an aide, Senator Jeffords requested that I meet him in his Senate office an hour later. I suffered alone for the next sixty minutes. At the appointed time, I was ushered into his inner chamber. Senator Jeffords—in his simple, low-key, balanced manner and with the tone and voice of a rural Vermonter devoid of Washington eloquence—told me that he was "tabling" this legislation because he believed that a comprehensive mental health parity bill was a better and necessary solution. I was gratified and appreciative of his stance, which for all intent and purpose killed this proposed legislation. In taking this action, the Senator wielded the power of the chair. Still, as a consequence, I know he incurred the wrath of many committee members and many organizations engaged in this debate.

Eight years later, a subsequent comprehensive parity bill, the Mental Health Parity and Addiction Equity Act, was passed and signed into law with Vermont's parity legislation of 1997 serving as the blueprint. Senator Wellstone's name accompanied the legislation, although he was killed in a tragic plane crash in 2002.

Thank you, Senator Jeffords, for "standing tall," adding my voice in the Senate chamber, and being an independent thinker.

A Booth in the Corner

The setting is not exactly a romanticized version of Casablanca as depicted in that classic movie made in 1942. In that iconic film, the central character, Rick, played by Humphrey Bogart, has several memorable lines.

The setting and location for this story is definitely not like the bustling, seductive gin joint pictured in the movie *Casablanca*. But sentiments expressed in this iconic film reverberate in profound and mysterious ways as I think about a special friendship that has enriched and warmed my life and heart.

"We'll always have the China Moon Buffet," I slyly said, with a crooked smile, to my good friend Steve as I slightly altered the tone and substance of Humphrey Bogart's sentimental line from *Casablanca*. We are both seated at this somewhat functional, most unpretentious restaurant in a local shopping mall on the Barre–Montpelier Road. Plates are piled high with Chinese food: rice and shrimp, chicken dishes, spareribs, and lo mein options served from vats filled with countless combinations from the expansive buffet.

Sitting across from me is a reserved, handsome, and good-hearted man. He and his lovely wife married young and raised three daughters. After years of teaching in the local school system, he retired early but not before carefully establishing a comfortable nest egg built on frugality and careful budgeting.

Behind his pleasant demeanor is a deeply embedded competitive nature. He is a man who "plays to win" whether at the local eatery or on the tennis court.

Not that I am immune to striving to be bigger and better.

Already I am aware, as Steve heads off for his second visit to the buffet line, that I am hard-pressed to keep up. It propels me to take another round of food starting with a generous portion of my favorite: General Tso's chicken. I am as much a food connoisseur as Steve is. And besides, remember I was the onetime recipient of the GOOD EATER AWARD at Public School 114 back in my elementary school days.

Steve grew up in a town and environment distinctly different from mine. My birthplace is Brooklyn, New York. Steve is a native of a smaller, more provincial burg: Montpelier, Vermont. Neither of us were kids when we met; we were both in our mid-fifties. From our first encounter, it was apparent that our differences in life experience, cultural background, political orientation, and personality served as a magnetic force that allowed us to bond in friendship rather than a barrier or roadblock.

Tennis would prove to be our significant common meeting ground although even in this sport, we were worlds apart. Steve not only learned the game early in life and had the form and grace of a tennis instructor, but it was a role he fulfilled over many years in various summer camps and schools. His strokes were smooth and clean, allowing him to place shots down the lines and in hidden corners. He moved around the court with grace, determination, and surprising speed even as the years passed.

My game consisted of self-taught, improvised, and slightly unreliable placement, but I relied on crafty strategic moves and natural athletic ability. Hitting soft drop shots over the net and lobbing balls deep became my calling card, which some opponents referred to as a torturous routine.

My tennis career began at age fifty when I decided to hang up my basketball sneakers. Steve and I started regularly playing a few years later. He was a fantastic tennis role model, but his approach was to give me on-the-court lessons. Despite my lack of experience and knowledge of the game, he insisted that we play formal matches every time we met. Just learning the scoring system was a challenge, and given Steve's competitive nature, I also learned how to keep an accurate account of final outcomes as we played. For over a year, I lost every match against an ace opponent.

As time progressed, I improved, our matches became more contested, and, on occasion, I came out on top. Best of all, our exchanges became louder and more expressive as we labored over intense, competitive play. According to others, our tennis matches became entertaining banter for those in range. While Steve never uttered a derogatory word, my language lacked a filter system. On occasion, Steve would stop playing and stomp off the court, claiming that my foul language was unsportsmanlike and unacceptable. Usually, he would return to the court and continue playing. I was contrite but unbowed. Apologizing, I would often reply, "Steve, I promise I won't say . . ." I'd then recite two or three of my most frequent "expletive deleted" words. Steve did not find this as funny as I did.

As was his nature, Steve was always on time or actually ten or fifteen minutes early for our matches. With neat tennis garb and hair combed into place, he could frame the cover of a tennis magazine while my outfits were more creative. I never missed a scheduled encounter, but my arrival was not as timely. One day, arriving later than intended, I frantically unloaded my sports bag in the locker room and discovered, with horror, that my tennis shorts were nowhere to be found. I ran out to tell Steve, who was displeased. "I will play in long pants," I replied. Steve said that was unacceptable.

"Give me five minutes to figure something out," I said and dashed off to the front desk at the tennis club. I appealed for help, and a kind soul guided me to a nearby room that housed a large lost-and-found box. Rummaging through, I found several shirts, loads of orphan socks, and several towels but only one pair of shorts. I grabbed them, went to the locker room, and quickly changed.

Steve took one look and started laughing. Before succumbing to uncontrolled glee, he said, "I can't believe this." Within a few seconds, he sank to the ground, leaning on all fours, hysterical with laughter and tears running down his handsome face. The truth was that my only option was to don a rather petite pair of pink shorts that some young woman must have misplaced and never reclaimed. Although we played the match to completion, Steve, the model of decorum, had to stop because he had trouble containing his laughter. Acting like a silly teenager was not his normal style. That afternoon, his laughter was infectious. It gave me a strange pleasure. Sharing laughter and joy offered us a unique way of building our relationship.

This episode left me slightly contrite, but as it turned out, it became the catalyst that led to our first lunch date. "You select the place," I said, assuming a friendly tone to make up for being unprepared earlier without proper tennis garb. Although I did not know Steve well then, I was aware that he was long retired and happy with that decision. I sensed that he was a frugal man—like me—so I was ever so pleased when he chose a local Chinese buffet over the high-end Topnotch Resort in Stowe or some fancy French place over in the Valley.

Steve, a creature of habit, picked a distant booth near the back corner of the dining room of the China Moon. From that day on, Steve would insist that we take that specific booth. It became such a ritual that upon seeing us enter, the waitstaff would escort us to our favored seats without a word. Steve, ever organized, always suggested we make lunch plans slightly before the noon hour since the place was relatively empty till midday. In a somewhat offbeat and bizarre way, this service and attention reminded me of how my favorite Aunt Billie—a woman of considerable means who ate out almost every night in New York City—was greeted and pampered by the attentive hosts in restaurants throughout lower Manhattan. In her honor, I even started calling the China Moon Buffet our lunch club.

I soon discovered that not only did we like each other but our many differences led to spirited and personal exchanges. His French-Canadian Catholic background fascinated me, and in turn, Steve enjoyed stories about my growing up with Jewish immigrant grandparents from the old country. And he showed curiosity, if not a touch of disdain, for adventures, misadventures, and experiences in my younger days in New York. Steve talked about his family and three daughters while I shared stories of my love life and my family in New Mexico. We had so much to talk about: politics, sports, the weather, aches and pains, and my new romantic relationships—with some competitive banter about who was more frugal.

From our very first lunch meeting, Steve always arrived early—usually ten minutes before I did—and he was already seated when I appeared. Without hesitation, when I entered the China Moon, I headed directly to our table in the corner booth. After a brief but friendly hello, we both made our way to the expansive food bar and loaded our plates from the abundant array.

Our lunch dates at the "club" were not weekly, but we made plans several times a month. Early in this new friendship, I arrived a few minutes early, and my new friend showered me with compliments for my attention to detail. Within minutes, we were ready to dig in. The food was most satisfying, but the company was even better. Being with Steve always made me feel better, and I would like to think that he felt the same way.

"Steve," I said in my best Bogart accent, pointing to him with a rather large egg roll in my hand, "hopefully, this is the beginning of a beautiful friendship." And so, it was.

A Boy and His Bike

The photograph sits in a large bin on top of a pile of slightly bent and discolored pictures up in the closet. The pile seemingly waits in eternity for further sorting and organizing or, in the worst case, for being deposited in a heap at the local dump.

There I am in this photo from the early 1950s, sitting on what appears to be a small brand-new one-speed bicycle, looking pleased and proud. Little did I know then about life, love, heartbreak, grand adventures, or the virtues of learning to ride a bike and how bike riding would change and enrich my life.

For many reasons, I intend to buy an appropriate picture frame and mount this "moment in time" on my office room wall. This will be a challenge given that unclaimed wall space at this point in my life is at a premium. Our house is filled with photos, keepsakes, and many objects of value; value measured in cherished memories rather than monetary worth. This is a condition not unknown to elderly couples aging in place.

For me and for many others, this experience—learning to ride a bike—was an absolute rite of passage, noted and applauded as another marker of growing up and gaining independence. I must have been eight or nine years old. As I recall, it was my father who ran behind and beside me as I wobbled my way up and down 127th Street in Rockaway. Little did I know that it would be one of his last special gifts to me because he died way too young, when I was twelve.

The unfolding of life remains a delicious mystery, and I seem to have managed without a well-defined or carefully developed script. In fact, for the first sixty-five years of my life, cycling was of limited importance or priority, although mastering the basics afforded me any number of special moments on my life resume, which is still being "updated" even in my seventy-eighth year.

The summer after my father's death, my mother signed me up for a bike trip on the island of Martha's Vineyard. While I was not consulted, the atmosphere at home was gloomy and depressive, so getting away for five days provided some respite. Our troop of twelve young riders, guided by two counselors from the New York YMCA, was bussed early in the morning to Woods Hole, Massachusetts, where we embarked on a ferry to the port of Vineyard Haven. Riding single file, we made our way to a hostel where we would sleep during our stay.

Later that very day, I was last in line as we traveled over hilly terrain, pedaling to the Gay Head cliffs on the very western edge of the island. The landscape was beautiful and lush green. Our first stop was in the village of Menemsha, and as we approached, we raced downhill into the quaint location, halting only when we reached the pier. Far from fearless, I remember pumping on my brakes as we swept downhill but with modest results.

The ride from there to Gay Head was both challenging and exhilarating. There was little flat terrain on the one curving, narrow road accentuated by ocean views and rolling waves off in the distance. Gay Head was a tiny village populated by descendants of the Wampanoag native tribe and an assortment of summer dwellers. The multicolored clay cliffs of Gay Head were a major attraction, rising more than one hundred feet from the rocky shoreline and the crashing waves below, rising steeply toward the historic, picturesque lighthouse.

The spectacular view could not mask my hesitancy and feelings of caution. Looking down from heights caused discomfort, and hiking up or down such terrain was not my favored activity. Despite my reluctance, I bowed to the peer pressure applied by the more adventurous teens on the trip. It was spearheaded by two teenage girls who, with almost reckless abandon, climbed down the steep clay cliffs and yelled for the rest of us to follow. I was the very last to descend as the waves smashed and pounded outsize rocks below and along the shore. It was frightening, exhilarating, and, in the end, an accomplishment for me, a timid young man. Climbing back up the clay cliffs was another challenge. I must admit I only looked up, not down the steep drop below. With a racing heart, I climbed up to the lighthouse parking lot and was reunited with the other bikers. Our reward was a visit to several nearby food shops in the shadow of the light beacon, affording us time for photographs of the lighthouse, the ocean, the colorful cliffs, and each other.

Returning to our bikes, we started pedaling east to our hostel ten miles away. I rode near the leaders, up toward the front of the pack, rather than hanging in the back.

Little did I know, but this early trip to Martha's Vineyard would resonate in later years when a shared family cottage in Gay Head provided opportunities for countless bike trips around all sections of this glorious island.

My access to cycling became important the following year when I secured my first summer job at the popular Boggiano's Bar and Grill across from Playland in Rockaway. I was fourteen, and it could be said I pedaled all summer long, transitioning from a kid into an adolescent. This means of transport afforded independence and an opportunity to travel back and forth from my house to Boggiano's with many unforgettable trips well past the midnight hour. On many a hot summer night at one in the morning, I rode along a boardwalk on the way home, guided by the ocean waves illuminated by the moon, steering clear of drunken teenagers looking for trouble.

That bike then sat mostly ignored and unused, sadly rusting away in the corner of our small garage.

Fourteen years passed until another bicycle played a significant role in my life. In 1971, in an improbable turn of events, I was accepted into a doctoral program at Harvard University.

Cambridge was an exciting and stimulating locale, and the opportunity was rich with promise and expectation. Being Ivy League had considerable appeal, but life still included mundane basic challenges like commuting to and from classes. Cambridge was bustling with hordes of people, heavy traffic, and a multitude of street performers on seemingly every corner. Most of my classes were held a mile or so from my apartment in an old, handsome colonial building, Nichols House, on a street named Appian Way on the Harvard campus.

With parking at a premium and congestion a challenge, cycling to and from classes offered a cheap and practical solution. A nearby sports shop in Inman Square provided me with my first three-speed cycle, a used bike with attractive red markings and several noticeable dents.

Traveling to and from classes was an adventure that included daily rides through the tumult of Harvard Square, the very heart of the city, filled with students, tourists, and townsfolk along with several lanes of confusing automobile traffic. There were no dedicated cycling lanes in the early 1970s, so bike commuting could be considered almost a contact sport. For five years, I rode my way in, around, and through the square ducking and dodging, weaving, and cruising. The process was not unlike my mostly successful attempts to meet all my course requirements at graduate school. Not only did I receive my doctorate, but I certainly improved my navigating and cycling skills during my years in Cambridge.

In 1976, I moved to the Green Mountains of Vermont. Within a month, I purchased an old farmhouse and ten acres of land on Sparrow Farm Road in East Montpelier. The setting was idyllic, but the house sat elevated more than thirteen hundred feet above the capital and the nearby Winooski River. Getting settled, I took note of the steep terrain between my place and downtown. To remind me of the elevation, my old Saab car literally wheezed its way home from town, chugging with effort as it climbed the last mile or two. When I departed Cambridge, I left many items behind but not my old, trusty—if slightly rusted and dented—red three-speed bicycle. It was tucked away unused.

Tommy, a precocious and curious young teenager living next door, knocked on my door that fall, and after some banter, asked me directly about my bike. He noticed that I had not used it the entire summer. He suggested that we make a trade. He offered to stack my wood for the coming winter and the following year in return for the bike. I liked his craftiness, and besides, the roads up to my house were a climb, one that I found not appealing. As I walked with him and his new acquisition, I reckoned that my cycling days were just about over.

It would be more than thirty-five years until I did any significant bike riding again, but when I did, I was taken with the experience. It was around the time I received my Medicaid card, so I guess you could say that I was maturing nicely. To celebrate, I purchased a used seven-speed bike from Onion River Sports in downtown Montpelier. This marked the beginning of a new chapter in my life, one marked by enhanced travel, adventure, exercise, and, of course, challenges. There was also an accident or two including an acrobatic but painful landing up in the Northeast Kingdom of Vermont.

Bike riding made me feel like a kid again, and on numerous cool but sunny spring days, I rode out to various downtown locations and beyond, getting acquainted with my bike. While in no way could I rival Major Taylor, a Black American cyclist who in 1899 became a world racing champion despite all odds and crushing racial discrimination, I managed to build my bike muscles and stamina as I rode along the Montpelier bike path out to the Three Mile Bridge, always pausing there for a view of the Winooski River.

I was not alone. Enhancing this endeavor was Sarah Hofmann, my new heartthrob, partner, and later-to-be wife. It was Sarah who inspired me to take up cycling. She was a powerful and tireless rider unafraid of challenges and backroads. On many trips, I trailed behind her and her attractive turquoise-blue two-wheeler, but I appreciated that she always kept me within sight in her rearview mirror.

It was not long until we began to explore bike trails further from the house. Frequently, we would load up our bikes and drive north on beautiful Route 12, past Elmore, and then stop in downtown Morrisville to commence cycling on a section of the rail trail. For nearly twenty miles, Sarah and I enjoyed the scenic views of farm pastures and cornfields as well as wooded, shaded forests that were most welcome on hot summer days. This trail extended all the way to Jeffersonville, pleasantly zigzagging along the Lamoille River with small bridges assisting us as we cycled past stunning mountain vistas.

A second gem, the Burlington Bike Path, became another favorite. Parking our car south of downtown, we rode through a Burlington waterfront that bustled with activity. Proceeding north for fifteen miles, we cycled past several parks and beaches, all augmented by spectacular views of Lake Champlain and the Adirondack Mountains. Since we saved the best for last, the ride ended after a three-mile sprint out on a narrow causeway, a path literally jutting out into Lake Champlain and offering dazzling sights in every direction.

Crossing bridges would become a common theme in our more distant explorations. I well remember approaching the ramp leading up to a larger bridge than the one over the Lamoille River. It was a steep climb as we pedaled up and over the Golden Gate Bridge in San Francisco on a cloudless day during a West Coast trip. As I cycled along, with Sarah leading the way, I tucked my fear of heights into an imaginary side pocket. I bravely glanced down, way down, at the rather huge tankers, pleasure boats, and sailboats that were directly below. Behind me and reflected off my little bike mirror was the impressive San Francisco skyline.

Certainly, more than a few bike trips had obstacles of note.

Some years ago, as we pedaled our way through the Everglades in Florida on a hot March day, we had to stop on occasion to ever-so-carefully navigate around objects blocking our way along a ten-mile bike path. The obstacles were an endless number of large alligators who obviously were attracted to the warmth offered on the asphalt path. At numerous points, we had to either cycle slowly around these reptiles or, in some instances, dismount ever so carefully and walk around these menacing predators. This was not a cycling trip for the faint of heart.

Other special bike experiences included a visit to Banff, Canada, on a late fall day. It was cold and snowing lightly when we called a local bike rental shop and were informed that they were closed although the owner who answered the phone was catching up on some paperwork. He relented and was so taken with our determination to cycle around Banff that he drove over to our hotel, the Caribou Lodge, and delivered two bikes. Sarah and I were dressed in layers, along with hats and gloves, as we cycled with spectacular northern Rocky Mountain peaks looming (literally hanging over us) at every turn. With light snow falling and a large herd of elk in view, we laughed like kids as we shook fresh flakes off our coats and made our way back to town.

On a pleasure trip to Paris, we spent five days on rented bikes, cycling to every section of the city, which allowed us to see not only countless historical sites, museums, and tourist attractions but some of the city's more diverse, colorful neighborhoods. Biking in a foreign country presents special challenges. Sarah and I were confused by various French street signs and directions. Somehow, we misread or misinterpreted directions to what we thought was a restricted bike lane, finding instead that we had entered a road reserved for motorcyclists, buses, tourist vans, and even garbage trucks. We did manage to survive, but later, over a glass of wine, we resolved that we might want to work on our French language skills before our next visit.

Over the past decade, we have taken several organized bike

tour trips to Europe and beyond. The first was to Italy, to the Puglia region, situated in the south and with a most appealing Mediterranean climate. Alas, on the first day of biking, my shoelace untied and became entangled in my pedal, but fortunately, no injuries were recorded. Our cycling participants had to stop while I made repairs. The only pain associated with this careless behavior was from my deflated ego and wounded pride. Then, for a week, we proceeded to glide along back roads, exploring the countryside filled with countless olive trees, stopping along the way in charming, ancient towns. We also rode to whitewashed hilltop villages and small cities sitting on the Adriatic Sea.

Two years later, on a bike trip to South Africa, we tested our bikes, riding under the magnificent Table Mountain in beautiful Cape Town and then around the southern tip of the continent, even pausing to park our bikes at the Cape of Good Hope for a special photo opportunity. We cycled around the scenic Cape Peninsula and then further into the countryside, making our way out to the Little Karoo region and the town of Oudtshoorn, which is the ostrich capital of the world. Biking near the Wartburg Mountains, we spent the night on a farm with well-prepared ostrich as the featured dish, aided by a carafe of delicious South African wine. As we made our way back to the Cape Town area, we cycled up and over a steep, narrow, winding mountain pass on a road without guardrails that climbed steadily for several miles without a break. This specific stretch was our most difficult and challenging mountain ride ever, but Sarah and I successfully cycled our way to the top, exhausted but exhilarated. It would not be an exaggeration to report that at the moment, we felt like we had just won the Tour de France.

A year or two later, we flew to Spain and toured in the Costa Brava region, pedaling along the Mediterranean Sea with reckless abandon. Besides the exotic seaside towns, we spent several days exploring Barcelona, one of the most appealing cities in the world.

In 2019, we took a trip to the biking paradise of Denmark and

Sweden, where cycling is a way of life. Even in large cities like Copenhagen and Stockholm, bike lanes guide the constant flow of cyclers with ease and safety. On one of our last days in Sweden, I recall, with joy and a sense of accomplishment, completing a forty-two-mile jaunt through the Swedish countryside. Sweden may lack mountains like the Alps, but from experience, I can confirm it has its share of steep rolling hills.

Despite or because of the pandemic of recent years, we aimed our sights on a domestic bike adventure. The fall of 2021 found us in Wyoming, where we toured the Tetons and Yellowstone National Park, assisted for the first time by electric bikes. We negotiated busy park roads, mountainous elevations, and stunning views. Our brakes came in handy when we rounded a corner and were confronted by the intrusion of a massive bison in our bike space during a glorious October week. Out of courtesy, if not caution, we waited for the beast to move before making a wide arc.

Not all bike trips were set in distant or exotic locales. One of our shortest trips was one of the most memorable. On an August day in 2017, Sarah and I rode less than a tenth of a mile, starting just above our house. We made a grand entrance by riding down the lawn adjacent to our homestead and rolled to a stop as we reached the old apple tree where our children and grandchildren were gathered anticipating a special occasion. Dismounting our bikes, we leaned them on the century-old tree and then stood together in full view as we exchanged our wedding vows.

At seventy-nine years of age, I find myself holding on tightly, perhaps too tightly, to these past cycling experiences, which seem to serve as a reminder of all my biking adventures. What started as a narrative of a boy and his bike has expanded to a lifetime of memories. With the anticipation of future cycling experiences still flickering and very much alive, this tale is not yet complete.

ACKNOWLEDGMENTS

I was not destined to be a young writing prodigy. By accident and chance, I started my quest to express myself in the written word at the ripe old age of seventy-four.

My literary career began when I spotted a sign in our local library with the word "FREE" on a poster. Since I was a frugal guy, I thought it worth my while to walk over and read the small print on the bulletin board. The announcement explained that as part of a writing program at a local college, a graduate student was fulfilling a requirement by offering four free introductory sessions focused on creative writing. On a whim, I joined this group without having experience, a plan, or expectations.

I was so uninformed that when I wrote my first short story in response to a prompt from the group's leader, I had no knowledge that I would be expected to read this piece to my group members the following week. I had assumed I would hand in this first sample to the facilitator and presumed that it would be returned with suggestions and corrections written in red ink.

As our second week gathering settled in, I was surprised, actually unnerved, when several group members were called upon to read their respective work. One woman shared a beautiful, long poem extolling the virtues of summer wildflowers. A second participant wrote about the importance of best friends, complete with an example or two. The next person tried to write a philosophical sketch about the meaning of life. It was a complex text and after a couple of minutes, my mind began to wander.

Imagine my discomfort and embarrassment when I was called on next to stand and read my story to this group of strangers. My small tome was not of a lofty subject matter. Still, it did include some scenes of a personal nature about sports, namely high school basketball and the relationship of a certain player with a stellar member of the school's cheerleading squad. As I concluded, I noticed several heads nodding affirmatively and recalled instances when I was interrupted by laughter and chuckling as my story unfolded.

Four sessions proved to be somewhat of a tease. Knowing that other group members had been writing for years, I felt like a true rookie, but I found comfort in sharing and telling stories. A friend mentioned that our local senior center sponsored writing workshops all year, and I was intrigued enough to join the Montpelier Senior Activity Center as a member and register for a writing class.

That is how I first met Maggie Thompson, a terrific local writing group facilitator in Central Vermont who became my mentor, teacher, and supporter. Maggie was like a wise, veteran sports coach who led not with aggressive posturing but with informed competence, kindness, and compassion. She created a safe environment for me and others in various writing groups over several years, and she provided encouragement, useful commentary, and, perhaps most importantly, a sense of endless possibilities. Instead of saying goodbye at the end of a session, she would emphatically sign off by saying, "Write on!"

In most facets of life, there are unsung heroes. For me, members of my local writing groups played that role. They taught me, through example, the power and wonder of creative writing. I came to appreciate the varying styles and voices in the storytelling process. Many written tales were personal, sometimes painfully so, but the willingness to reveal real-life experiences moved me greatly. Other stories were laced with lightness and humor, resulting in smiles and laughs. From my peers, I learned how impactful it is to write and share personal stories. Within a year, I was convinced that everyone had a story to tell.

Carla Occaso played an outsized role in promoting my fledgling writing career just as it hit the first-year mark. Carla, who lived a short way down from my house, stopped on her way home on a September afternoon. She pulled her car over so we could chat and catch up. I told her about my participation for one year in a local writing group and mentioned that I had several short story memoirs completed. Besides being a teacher, Carla was the editor of the *Montpelier Bridge*, a local community paper with an expanding circulation. She asked me to drop a story or two in her mailbox. I had no real expectations but hoped she would give me feedback. Carla appreciated and enjoyed my work; the *Montpelier Bridge* carried seven original stories, including several on the front page over the next twelve months. This exposure was surprising and unexpected, acting as sort of a booster shot in my early literary efforts.

My wife, Sarah Hofmann, never wavered in supporting this endeavor. Without her good cheer, advice, and technical expertise, my book would be little more than a random pile of papers in a basement bin. Sarah was encouraging from the start, reassuring, and the very definition of a true companion. During moments of uncertainty and despair, the low moments were related not to my writing but the challenges of my shortcomings with computer technology. Sarah supplied endless patience and good cheer, making this book a labor of love.

The encouragement from family and friends deserves mention, along with the loving and loyal response of my son Jamie, who gave positive reviews to various drafts of stories that were in early form and far from complete.

The good folks at, or connected to, Rootstock Publishing, namely owner Samantha Kolber, Stephen McArthur, and editor Kathleen Champlin, were essential to this book. They took me on an unexpected journey from a manuscript to a cherished collection of published essays.

   Thank you all.

Thanks also to the following newspapers where some of these essays, in earlier forms, were first published:

"Good Eater," *Montpelier Bridge*, September 16, 2020

"A Love Affair Revealed," *Montpelier Bridge*, February 17th 2021

"From Ebbets Field to the Montpelier Rec," *Montpelier Bridge*, May 18, 2021

"Coming of Age at Boggiano's Bar and Grill," *Montpelier Bridge*, August 10, 2021

"Ralph Geer," *Montpelier Bridge*, November 16, 2021

"The Big Picture on Big Pharma," *Montpelier Bridge*, January 26, 2022

"March Madness, Montpelier Style," *Montpelier Bridge*, March 8, 2022

"Uniting the World," *Barre-Montpelier Times Argus*, November 19, 2022

ABOUT THE AUTHOR

Ken Libertoff was born in Brooklyn, New York, on a snowy day on January 16, 1945. His grandparents, Jewish immigrants, settled in Crown Heights and Bensonhurst.

Ken grew up in Rockaway, Queens where he attended public schools. His academic achievements at Far Rockaway High School were modest compared to his athletic prowess on the basketball court. His resume, which included being captain of the team for two years and membership on the All-Queens first team roster, certainly did not hurt his chances of being accepted at the University of Connecticut. Ken played on championship varsity teams in the mid-1960s.

His adolescent years at home were marred by the death of his father when Ken was twelve and the realization that his mom, a woman who would live a full life until age ninety-five, was confronted with serious lifetime mental health challenges. He and his younger sister, Karen, persevered.

Upon graduation in 1966, Ken had a narrow window of interest and little sense of direction. He considered a career in college coaching. This changed when a chance meeting occurred with a dynamic, young psychology professor at Yale who recognized something special in him and convinced Ken to settle in New Haven.

For the next five years, Ken became politically engaged, working in several war-on-poverty projects in the city's most troubled neighborhoods, including a model residential program for delinquent kids. He also served as a research assistant in Yales's Psychology Department. Several Yale faculty members and community members encouraged Ken to pursue further educational opportunities. In an improbable and unexpected turn of events, he was accepted at the only program he applied to, the Clinical Psychology and Public Practice doctoral program at Harvard University.

Finishing all his coursework in early 1976, Ken, his wife, and newborn son Jamie moved to Montpelier, Vermont. While writing his dissertation on runaway children, he also directed the local youth bureau. Two years later, Ken celebrated the completion of his doctorate in 1978.

In 1981, he was named director of a small statewide non-profit, the Vermont Association for Mental Health, which he built up over three decades. His advocacy at the Vermont Statehouse on behalf of mental health, substance abuse treatment, and children's services was recognized and applauded with numerous awards, such as: State Advocate of the Year, for passage of Vermont's Parity Legislation in 1997; Behavioral Healthcare Tomorrow Award for successfully fighting for comprehensive insurance coverage for people with mental illness in 2002; the Jack Barry Communications Award for Excellence in Advocating for Recovery Centers presented by Friends of Recovery in 2010; Citizen of the Year Award presented by Vermont Medical Society in 2010; and the Lifetime Legendary Leadership Award, presented by Mental Health America in 2010.

Ken retired in 2010, but not before meeting the love of his life, Sarah Hofmann, a local lawyer who, in addition to being a noted utility regulator in Vermont, was a smart, funny, kind, and adventurous person. They married in 2017. In 2019, on a whim, Ken joined a small, local writing group and began a new endeavor. Without a plan or purpose, he started his literary career believing, "we all have a story to tell."

More Nonfiction from Rootstock Publishing:

A Peek Under the Hood: Heroin, Hope, & Operation Tune-Up
   by Michael Pevarnik
A Judge's Odyssey by Dean B. Pineles
A Lawyer's Life to Live by Kimberly B. Cheney
Alzheimer's Canyon: One Couple's Reflections on Living with Dementia
   by Jane Dwinell & Sky Yardley
Attic of Dreams: A Memoir by Marilyn Webb Neagley
Catalysts for Change ed. by Doug Wilhelm
China in Another Time by Claire Malcolm Lintilhac
Circle of Sawdust: A Circus Memoir of Mud, Myth, Mirth, Mayhem and Magic
   by Rob Mermin
Collecting Courage: Anti-Black Racism in the Charitable Sector
   eds. Nneka Allen, Camila Vital Nunes Pereira, & Nicole Salmon
Cracked: My Life After a Skull Fracture by Jim Barry
I Could Hardly Keep From Laughing by Don Hooper & Bill Mares
Nobody Hitchhikes Anymore by Ed Griffin-Nolan
Notes from the Porch by Thomas Christopher Greene
Pauli Murray's Revolutionary Life by Simki Kuznick
Preaching Happiness by Ginny Sassaman
Red Scare in the Green Mountains by Rick Winston
Save Me a Seat! A Life with Movies by Rick Winston
Striding Rough Ice: Coaching College Hockey and Growing Up In the Game
   by Gary Wright
Tales of Bialystok: A Jewish Journey from Czarist Russia
   by Charles Zachariah Goldberg
The Atomic Bomb on My Back by Taniguchi Sumiteru
The Language of Liberty by Edwin C. Hagenstein
The Last Garden by Liza Ketchum
The Morse Code: Legacy of a Vermont Sportswriter by Brendan Buckley
Uncertain Fruit: A Memoir of Infertility, Loss, and Love
   by Rebecca & Sallyann Majoya
Walking Home: Trail Stories by Celia Ryker
You Have a Hammer: Building Grant Proposals for Social Change
   by Barbara Floersch

Learn about our Fiction, Poetry, and Children's titles at
www.rootstockpublishing.com.

Printed in the USA
CPSIA information can be obtained
at www.ICGtesting.com
JSHW021126311223
54545JS00001B/3

9 781578 691579